D1329431

Praise for

The Revolutionary Guide to Acting

April Webster, *Emmy Award–Winning Casting Director*—Star Wars: Episode VII, Star Trek Beyond.

"In the many years that I have known and also taught with Bernard, I have witnessed many actors and others that have attended his Master-classes undergo amazing transformations. His book has insights that have helped artists attain success as well as a healing of the heart."

Costa Ronin, *Actor*—Homeland, The Americans, Once Upon a Time in Hollywood.

"Bernard has had a tremendous influence on my career. Studying with him enabled me to reach and understand the deepest of human emotions through the study of self. It is because of his intimate understanding of human nature and its relation to storytelling that I see my personal and professional life as before and after I started working with Bernard. I will be forever grateful for his guidance."

Bruce Dern, *Actor, Two Time Academy Award Nominee*

"Bernard has the courage to develop the best acting class in America. I haven't seen something like this in 50 years!"

David Oyelowo, *Actor*—Selma, Star Wars: Rebels

"I see that you don't do this work for money, I can see, that acting is at the core of who you are!"

David Dinerstein, *Academy Award–Winning Producer*—Summer of Soul, A Private War, Kidnap

"Acting is about dedicating your heart and soul to something that is greater than yourself. It is what I have done with my life as a producer, and this book will inspire and teach you to do the same."

Shira Haas, *Actress*—Unorthodox, Shtisel.

"I remember the first time we talked, and Bernard told me about the meaning of being grateful and the power in believing in miracles. I remember how blown away I was by that. It made me realize that not only is he a brilliant advisor and talented artist, but he is also a sensitive, compassionate, and humble human being. He has the most excellent combination of being professional and delicate—stubborn, yet thoughtful—a perfectionist but also empathetic."

Fernando Cayo, *Actor*—La Casa de Papel (Money Heist).

"Working with Bernard is an experience that an artist cannot miss. Bernard's exercises and methods are transformative, as they work on your conscious and subconscious. His techniques enter your hard drive and change your destructive and limiting beliefs. Your negative fearful experiences will disintegrate, and you'll connect with your heart, making you a better actor and a better human being."

Joanna Kulig, *Actress*—Cold War, Hansel & Gretel: Witch Hunters.

"Acting is an art of living. To act and to live, you need to have courage. To get courage you must develop yourself every day. Having inspiring people around you, like mentors and coaches, is crucial. You should learn their techniques and methods through classes or personal meetings. Reading this amazing book is the next best idea. When you read *The Revolutionary Guide to Acting* you will get better every day."

Carlos Bardem, *Actor*—Scorpion in Love, Assassin's Creed.

"Bernard's classes are totally unique! A space for experimentation in freedom and ideal to feed what you need most in acting: imagination and creativity."

Dan Hubbard, *Casting Director*—King Kong, Downton Abbey.
"Bernard is a tsunami of knowledge, advice, positive energy, razor-sharp direction, and foresight. Having worked with the most talented and well-known actors, producers and directors in the industry, Bernard is a star in his own right. He has an encyclopedic wealth of knowledge and he not only teaches with his powerful mind but has a heart of gold shining through in his work and teachings. I have never met anyone like him!"

THE
REVOLUTIONARY
GUIDE
^{TO} ACTING

THE REVOLUTIONARY GUIDE TO ACTING

BECOME THE ARTIST YOU WERE BORN TO BE

BERNARD HILLER

Matt Holt Books
An Imprint of BenBella Books, Inc.
Dallas, TX

The Revolutionary Guide to Acting copyright © 2022 by Bernard Hiller

All rights reserved. No part of this book may be used or reproduced in any manner whatsoever without written permission of the publisher, except in the case of brief quotations embodied in critical articles or reviews.

Matt Holt is an imprint of BenBella Books, Inc.
10440 N. Central Expressway
Suite 800
Dallas, TX 75231
benbellabooks.com
Send feedback to feedback@benbellabooks.com

BenBella and *Matt Holt* are federally registered trademarks.

Printed in the United States of America
10 9 8 7 6 5 4 3 2 1

Library of Congress Control Number: 2022935021
ISBN 9781637742204 (hardcover)
ISBN 9781637742211 (electronic)

Copyediting by Michael Fedison
Proofreading by Lisa Story and Michael Fedison
Text design and composition by Aaron Edmiston
Cover design by Bernard Hiller Production
Cover photography by Taili Song Roth
Printed by Lake Book Manufacturing

Special discounts for bulk sales are available.
Please contact bulkorders@benbellabooks.com.

In Loving Memory of a True Hero
Hershel Schuster
1922–2020

CONTENTS

FOREWORD

I have always had an aversion to writing the foreword for a book, and, fortunately, I'd never been asked. But when Bernard Hiller called and asked me to write one, I quickly said yes and then politely asked him to remind me who he was. He assumed I was kidding. So I googled him, and I immediately recalled that he was the world-famous acting coach and motivator, and that I'd known him for years.

Bernard makes me happy. He is the kind of guy who you wish would follow you around all day so that when you sagged, he would be there to pick you up. The first time I met him he was so unfailingly positive that I looked into having him roughed up. By the tenth time we crossed paths, I finally had to admit he is the real deal. Bernard is inspired and inspiring. He is a natural motivator and yet he's not really about motivation at all. Simply put, Bernard teaches truth-telling, which, as it turns out, is what acting, and probably all art and most of life, are in fact all about.

When you watch a movie, see a play, or look at a painting and you recognize something truthful, that's good art! When you read a book and go, "Oh yeah," to something that you hadn't thought of but recognize because you've seen it a thousand times, that's art! Even broad comedies have to have a sliver of truth in them to work. No matter how stupid or misguided or wrong a character's actions might be, if you believe that that character would do that at that time, then it's honest, and the viewers can lose themselves in the story.

I feel this book is not just for actors or artists, but for everyone! Whether you are a junior in art school or a fifty-year-old partner at a Big Four accounting firm. Bernard knows that, no matter what you do in life, self-honesty and authenticity are the core to happiness and success. Yet being honest with yourself is hard. When you're honest, you put your true self and, more problematically, your ego on the line. You feel fear because you risk failing at something that really matters to you. Unfortunately, most people put aside their dreams and goals because they can't handle this fear.

Bernard understands that this fear is the great separator. It is the enemy of truth, and his techniques help you overcome that. Those of you who have the courage to NOT protect your egos, to face fear head-on, and who are honest about your desires . . . only YOU have the ability to create great things. This book will make your journey easier.

Peter Farrelly—Two-time Oscar Winner,
Director for Best Picture, *Green Book*

Los Angeles International Masterclass.
Photo: Peter Augustin

WHY I WROTE THIS BOOK
& WHY YOU NEED IT

"TO BE, OR NOT TO BE?"

This is Shakespeare's most piercing question, and people have been grappling with it for the past five hundred years. I imagine that "the slings and arrows of outrageous fortune" that he so vividly describes were the many challenges he faced in his own personal life as well as what he experienced as an artist. This is the profound life-changing question that every one of us asks ourselves, consciously or subconsciously.

Are you willing to have the courage to overcome your doubts, blocks, and fears to become the person you must be so that you may live out your dreams and goals, or are you surrendering to the negative crowd that tells you how to live your life, that suffering will inevitably become your future, reminding you that you're not good enough, to play small, hide your gifts, and live your life in shame?

There comes a moment in your life when you need to DECIDE to . . .

REMAIN OR CHANGE?

HIDE OR SHINE?

LIVE OR DIE?

"In this world, the most difficult thing you'll ever have to become—is the real you!"

If you have decided that you want to be truly SPECTACULAR, then this is the book for you!

Let me be your guide on this incredible journey! I have been in show-business for almost thirty-eight years. I started out as a teenage performer, putting in years of preparation, passion, and persistence to excel at this very demanding and artistic profession. I have now been teaching my Masterclasses, seminars, and success workshops around the globe for the past twenty-two years.

I will be forever grateful for all the gifts that acting training has brought me and for making me become the person that I always wanted to be and more. I have also included updates to the methods and exercises that I wrote about in my first book, *Stop Acting, Start Living.*

This book contains revolutionary acting techniques and exercises, which have transformed the lives of hundreds of thousands of actors, singers, performers, and business leaders around the world. You will also learn unique success techniques that will help you to surpass your goals and dreams. These methods will work with anyone who has a passionate, open heart and a hunger for a sensational career and life. They will transform you into a powerful and emotionally connected human being. When you reach this state of being, anything you desire in showbusiness or any other profession is possible!

Finally, you'll be able to start living the creative and artistic life that was truly meant for you and become the actor everyone wants to work with!

It's time for YOU to learn the secrets that superstars and professional actors know and make a bigger impact on your career.

The most important thing I discovered on my journey to becoming an artist is that I really needed to connect with my authenticity, my talent, and my instincts. I call this the "Journey Toward Yourself." Finding my true self gave me the knowledge and power to create performances that affected an audience. It took a long time, but it also changed me in ways I could never have imagined.

No matter what you pursue in life, the ultimate indicator of your success is not just from your skill set or experiences—it's YOU—the human being! To succeed, you need to become a fully open, positive-thinking, happy, powerful, and emotional human being. These characteristics are not easy to acquire, but nothing great has ever been easily achieved. As a teacher, I have been impressed by students and artists who have experienced difficult obstacles in their life and still manage to succeed.

Since you were born, you have received messages from the world around you. Maybe you were told to play it safe, to hide, not to take risks, not to feel, and you became numb to your own pain and suffering. This will lead you into a comatose state. Many people are in a coma, where they are emotionally and spiritually dead but have their eyes open. When you are in this state, only a major crisis will wake you up! Having a crisis in your life can actually be very good for you! It can help you get out of your comfort zones, which are bankrupting and destroying your soul.

> **"If you're unconscious, your future is created by your limited past. If you are conscious, your future is created by your actions and intentions."**

To be successful in this business, you will need to become an expert in human skills. Be connected and be able to communicate your feelings. Be emotionally invested in your dreams or goals and inspire others with your passion and ideas. These skills are essential and vital to your success. You will have to understand the psychology, sociology, and emotional capacity of human beings better than anyone. In order to do that, you must first discover the TRUTH about yourself!

Giving unforgettable performances and having a successful career can only occur when you are strongly connected to the AUTHENTIC YOU! Being fake, dishonest, pretending, or "acting" is the total opposite of what is now required. If we see that you are "acting" in any way, you will not have a long future in the Hollywood film and TV industry. You will quickly become irrelevant because the industry doesn't like tricksters, deceivers, or liars. They want the real deal. THE TRUTH.

Nowadays, acting is accessing the parts of *yourself* that pertain to that particular character. The audience shouldn't be able to distinguish between you and the person you are playing. Actors speak their dialogue not only with words, but also with their body, thoughts, and soul.

> *"The camera can film my face, but until it captures*
> *my soul, you don't have a movie." —Al Pacino*

You must create a powerful and unique performance for the viewer to be interested and inspired by what you have to say and for other professionals to want to work with you. To become good at that, one way would be by expressing your special qualities in your life, not just onstage or in front of a camera. Being authentic will help you attract the right people for your journey. You can't fake it. No matter how convincing your words may be, your body never lies.

In life, we analyze facial expressions and the physical body to see if someone is telling us the truth or not. It's one of the reasons why, at our studio, we do a great deal of work on connecting the actor with their body. Learning to emotionally connect with your acting partner is also not an easy task. The capacity for empathy and understanding someone other than yourself is a skill that takes time to develop, but it all starts with wanting to find and understand the real you!

THE ACTING LOVER

"Acting is like a 'lover' that you will have to live with for the rest of your life. Always protect your lover!" —Tom Hanks

Loving someone is an act of faith because you don't know what the future holds. As Tom said, "Acting is like a lover . . ." It demands your constant attention, passion, and commitment to making it work.

Ask yourself, are you willing to share your feelings, emotions, and life experiences with acting? You will need to use them in the characters that you play.

Your "acting lover" will keep testing your level of dedication. Be aware that if you don't show your commitment to them, they will find someone else who will. Connecting once in a while is not enough to show them how serious you are about this "relationship." You must show *evidence* to convince your "acting lover" that you are sincere and that this is important to you. If this "acting affair" fails, it's because you didn't show enough attention, hard work, or dedication to your "acting lover."

Actions you must do to show that you are serious about this relationship:

1. You schedule a meeting with your "acting lover" to build a stronger connection several times a week.

2. You keep learning, growing, and transforming in order to become a better version of yourself—for your "acting lover."

3. You keep creating new opportunities to be able to spend more time with them.

4. You bring passion, love, and joy to everything you do, to inspire your "acting lover" to want to work with you.

Spending time with your "lover" brings a great deal of value, excitement, and meaning. So, without sharing your talent, acting would be losing out on the artistic love story of a lifetime!

CHAPTER 1

ACTING IS A "LIVING" PROBLEM

Shakespeare put it best: "All the world's a stage, and all the men and women merely players."

There's not a single day that goes by that we are not using *acting* to play different "roles" in our daily lives. We go from playing a father to a doctor, from a mother to an executive, even from a student to a performer. We are all playing different parts of ourselves, but without powerful training, exploration, and transformation, you will never be able to play these roles to their full extent. Each part we play has different requirements, and you'll switch from one part to another throughout your day. Now, how well you play each individual part will determine your success in life.

The moment a family's first baby is born is the moment that someone is given the "parent" role. These new parents are usually not well versed on how to play these roles effectively. They are simply copying what they have witnessed before. Now, parents who decide to prepare for these roles by learning and studying will, of course, do much better.

Some children become extremely disappointed with their parents because, according to them, the parents didn't play the part as perfectly as the children believe they should have. This may be how you feel toward your parents, but did you play your part as their son or daughter as perfectly as they thought you should have played it? Maybe, or maybe not.

When those expectations aren't met, it leads to feelings of anger, sadness, disconnection, and frustration. If these feelings are continuously unaddressed, they will block you from fully playing powerful roles in the future.

During childhood, many become connected to the weakest part of themselves, which is why they don't succeed in showbusiness or any other business. To pursue acting successfully, you must first connect to the most powerful version of yourself.

In the acting-teaching circle, there's a common misconception that having a lot of traumatic experiences in your life is desired because you can use them in your work. Well, this would be true if you were on top of your personal problems, but if your personal problems are on top of you, then you can't use them because, *at this moment,* they're using you! Only when you successfully work through your issues will you be able to use your difficult past experiences in your work.

If you want to be extraordinary in any role you play, you must become what I like to call a "professional" human being. The reason professional people achieve their goals is due to their hunger for learning, focused and consistent practice, and willingness to do whatever it takes to reach their peak performance. They also ask for help and are willing to face and overcome the obstacles and challenges that are put in front of them.

"If you want to remain strong, ask for help." —*Les Brown*

Unfortunately, most people remain "amateurs" for their entire lives. Amateurs never actively pursue their dreams or deal with the personal or professional issues that are stopping them. They also never invest in their glorious future of possibilities, and so their brilliance will lie dormant inside of them—forever!

Just imagine that you are the most powerful electronic machine in the world. What happens if you can't find an electrical outlet? You're useless, right? It is your responsibility to find your power supply to plug yourself into. When you are fully connected, you will discover your talents, gifts, instincts, and purpose. Professionals know that they need to connect to their energy force in order to succeed.

"Successful people do what unsuccessful people are not willing to do." —*Jim Rohn*

"When you are truly connected to yourself, you are connected to life's possibilities."

CHAPTER 2

YOUR LIFE IS YOUR ART

"Art enables us to find ourselves and lose ourselves
at the same time." —Thomas Merton

Our culture lacks a depth of soul; it's the artist's purpose to bring the soul back into the world. Life is crying out to you, revealing something glorious about itself in every moment. So pay attention to nature, humanity, poetry, music, art, ballet, opera, and theatre. Listen and watch carefully, and don't let notable moments go by unappreciated or unnoticed.

"Fall in love with art, the way art expresses life."

"Art is the means by which we communicate what
it feels like to be alive." —Antony Gormley

"True actors or artists never need outside motivation to keep growing and training."

True actors will do whatever it takes to keep creating because they have an artistic soul that's on fire. It is something they're working on every day, and they're not waiting for anyone's permission. Acting is one of the most wonderfully expressive and compassionate art forms in the world. It's about sharing all different parts of yourself with others, and there is nothing more courageous and vulnerable than that. If you're fortunate enough to feel that you were born to be creative, consider yourself lucky.

"Only creativity allows progress to occur."

I tell students, "Real actors know that acting is not a choice. You don't choose it; it chooses you!" Having been blessed to be an actor, singer, dancer, director, producer, screenwriter, and acting trainer for the past thirty-eight years, I have discovered that genuine actors, performers, and artists have this performing gene. It's in their blood, their DNA. You become an actor or performer not because you want to but because you have to!

Now, if you come into the acting profession seeking to find fortune or fame, you will fail. However, if you want to be a part of a profession that brings you meaning and purpose, you will inevitably create a career for years to come. The industry welcomes you!

This profession is for those who love learning about themselves and are truly fascinated by life and all that it entails. It is also for those who want to learn and understand a variety of relationships and people that are different from themselves.

Remember, success and fulfillment are what you give yourself. Fame and fortune are what others give you. Acting, more than any other art form, has given the world a deeper understanding of and compassion for fellow human beings. It fosters connections and develops empathy with others. During crises and tragedies, people look to leaders in the artistic community for entertainment, comfort, and reflection. Throughout history, performers have been there to raise spirits, give hope, and bring people together.

A wonderful actor once sent me a humbling note that I will never forget:

> *"I just want to tell you, that your work is much more important than acting itself. It's taught me how to connect to my true self. There I found my gifts, my passion, my purpose, and myself. And, for that, I will be forever grateful."*—Michael Stromme

> *"Theatre is the art of looking at ourselves."* —Augusto Boal

CHAPTER 3

THE DIFFERENCE BETWEEN AN ACTOR & AN ARTIST

I get asked, "What's the difference between an actor and an artist?" I tell them, "It's the difference between legendary and easily forgettable performances!"

An *actor* is someone who looks at a part or role and does what the writer or screenwriter expects of them. They play the scene exactly as it is written. If the scene calls for crying—they cry. If it calls for yelling—they yell. Many fine actors work this way, and they give you precisely the performance you would expect them to give. It's also known as *playing it safe*. I feel that these actors are not fully exploring their creativity, instincts, or uniqueness within the role. Stella Adler once said, "Actors need a kind of aggression, a kind of inner force. Don't be only one-sided, sweet, nice, good. Get rid of being *average*." And, "Find the *artistic killer* in you."

Now *artists*, on the other hand, are the actors who dare to be different and give you the unexpected. They will always surprise you with their performance and the choices they make. Once you see them in the part they're playing, you can't think of anyone else playing that role. It becomes definitive! They act in unpredictable ways because they are always making interesting and unexpected choices when playing their character. Therefore, you're unable to take your eyes off of them because you never know what they're about to do next.

The artist looks at a scene and thinks, *How can I bring my intention, passion, and emotion to the scene, but in a completely original, new, and unique way?* They know that the script provided to them is not the whole truth. (Read chapter fourteen: "Dare to Be Different!")

The word *artist* also applies to many different professions including singer, composer, musician, director, cinematographer, costume designer—to mention only a few. We use this word when someone stands apart from the rest and brings us something that makes us go "WOW." (Read chapter ten: "It's the 'Wow' Factor.")

> **"Artists bring light into darkness, hope into despair, and give love where there is hate."**

Think about any artist that you love in any field. You connect with them because they're special, unique, one of a kind, and they affect you as no other artist does. They brought you something that you had never experienced before. However, being different does sometimes bring a great deal of criticism, but it doesn't stop them!

An artist is someone who makes a lasting impression on society, like Mozart, Shakespeare, Baryshnikov, da Vinci, Austen, Pavarotti, or Sondheim. You'll never forget them, and their unique artistry stays with you forever. These artists profoundly touched my soul.

For me, the genuine artists that I have seen, known, or worked with have inspired me and made me understand life in a completely different way.

Focus on becoming an *artist* no matter what profession you're in. To be astonishing, you must explore the land of the unknown. Artists are seizing new ground and working without a map. Right now, more than ever, the world needs the artist in YOU to step forward. Invest in yourself and become the artist that is inside of you, and you might encourage others to take risks and discover their true selves!

> **"Don't settle for being ordinary when you could be EXTRAORDINARY!"**

CHAPTER 4

WHY MOVIES ARE IMPORTANT

"Art is a lie that makes us realize the truth." —*Pablo Picasso*

Films can transform us. They can educate and inspire us so profoundly that we change our lives because of them. They serve an important function in our society.

"Creativity is the essence of life."

So, why do people love watching movies?

1. To hear and see the truth about life and ourselves. It's human nature to want to see others who look and behave like us, and as a result, we identify with them on the screen and are reminded that we are all part of the same human race. Other cultures, languages, religions, and countries emphasize

21

our differences, but the performing arts acknowledge our commonality. So, when a character's heart is breaking in the story, we weep with them because we know what heartbreak feels like. It's also true that watching people who are not like us helps us connect and grasp a deeper understanding of our own existence.

Bring seven hundred people from different backgrounds together into a movie theatre to watch *Romeo and Juliet*, and when the lovers die, everyone feels sad, no matter what part of the world they are from. They may not understand the language the film was spoken in, but everyone in the world understands love, pain, and loss.

Every generation must struggle with constructing their own identities and learning how to deal with life, love, relationships, sex, trauma, death, and the world around them. By watching films, they can see how other people deal with these issues and problems, which helps them view and understand their own situation differently.

"Every baby is born with a cry for help." —Cornel West

2. To see beauty. Movies take us to magnificent foreign lands and to exotic and mysterious places without ever having to leave the safety of our comfy seats.

3. To connect with others. Watching something alone doesn't have the same effect. It's a special and unique experience to watch a film with a large and passionate live audience. This

is a shared experience that you can't replicate in your own home.

4. To see people who are willing to stand out and be different, refusing to let the "crowd" dissuade them from their actions, ideas, dreams, or opinions. Many films have been made about regular people who finally decided to let their true selves be seen and heard, no matter the consequences. Those characters aren't listening to the crowds anymore. They're listening to their inner voice.

5. To laugh. We all need an escape from the stress, difficulties, and pain in our lives. One minute of laughter actually boosts your immunity for twenty-four hours. Laughter truly is the best medicine!

6. To feel hopeful. When movies have a happy ending, it gives us a feeling that anything is still possible. You believe that no matter how terrible things appear to be, one can still succeed.

    Watch *It's a Wonderful Life*, and you'll know what I'm talking about.

"Once you choose hope, anything's possible." —*Christopher Reeve*

7. To experience vocal and physical freedom. We see characters singing and dancing in the rain. If you haven't already seen it, watch the classic musical film *Singin' in the Rain*, starring Gene Kelly. Some of my other favorite musical films you should watch are *An American in Paris*, *Funny Girl*, and *The*

Band Wagon. These films encourage us to show ourselves through song and dance, not just our words.

8. To see creativity in action. When we see classic movies like *Star Wars* and *Indiana Jones*, or even animated films like *Toy Story*, they show us the ability and the unlimited imagination of the creative mind. *Art begins when you use your creativity.* You will need to use your creativity to help turn "your dreams into reality." I recently read a book that predicted what future employers will be looking for. It states that in the future there will be AI machines able to memorize anything a person can learn or know, but creativity, instinct, and imagination are impossible for them to replicate. These innate and natural human skills will be the most important factors for our future employment.

9. To see people being emotional and vulnerable. Most people are disconnected or blocked from their own feelings and are unable to express their emotions. This is a major problem. We see actors expressing their most intimate feelings and showing us what we must do to truly feel alive.

10. We learn the most important of all lessons—ROMANCE! What we all know about love, relationships, and sex we have learned from watching movies. It's true! Think back to the first time you saw kissing or affection of any kind; you either saw your parents or more likely you saw it in . . . a film or on a TV show. It also shapes the way we understand romantic rituals and dating behaviors. Films play a vital role in the understanding and enhancing of our romantic sensibility.

Great films also challenge and influence worldly culture and societal norms, adding their wisdom and insight into issues such as injustice and prejudice. Many powerful films also advocate for a world with greater understanding, tolerance, empathy, and love toward one another.

In a way, your life is like a movie. It's conceived, written, produced, and starring you!

What kind of movie are you in? Is it a tragedy, a drama, a comedy, or a fantasy? Maybe it's a horror movie? Here's an idea. Why not star in a film about triumph, excitement, and love? I really like that one!

Or maybe STAR in a movie you actually want to experience and live! Well, for that to happen, you may need to make significant changes, because, believe it or not . . . *"Your life is a movie you can create every day."*

CHAPTER 5

STOP HIDING & START SEEKING

There is a famous children's game called hide-and-seek. I'm sure you know it. It's when players have to run away to find a good hiding spot, while another player closes their eyes and counts to ten—and then seeks the others out. It's a fun game for a child, but the problem is many of you are playing it as adults. That's when this game sadly becomes tragic.

You're hiding, hoping that someone will find and uncover the real you. What you fail to realize is that *no one is looking for you*, and you are actually playing this game all by yourself. You're either too afraid to ask for advice or too scared to put yourself out there. You hope that eventually someone will magically find you and realize how talented you are. You're also staying hidden because you're afraid that if someone does find you, then you just won't be good enough. These thoughts kill careers and eventually damage your life.

This type of thinking comes from experiencing a difficult or somewhat traumatic past where you may have been bullied, criticized, ridiculed, or even ostracized when you spoke out or were seen. It was then that you decided to become an expert "hider" in this game we call "life" because it would be too painful to be *found*. This is a huge mistake!

> **"You should know that hiding your true self is at the root of all suffering."**

STOP DOING THAT IMMEDIATELY!

It takes an enormous amount of energy to keep hiding, and when you don't allow yourself to be seen or heard, you will never discover your life's purpose. So, by hiding, you are in fact inflicting much more pain upon yourself. When you hide your talent, ideas, dreams, feelings, passion, and abilities, you hide who you truly are. Don't shun your unique magnificence! Without showing us your genuine, multilayered self, you become just another statistic instead of someone uniquely special that could contribute to the betterment of humankind. The world *does* need your talent.

In order to have a successful career, you will need people in the industry to see your gifts! In life, the only things you can ever do alone are to be sad or fail. You must put yourself in a position to have your talents seen and discovered before anything great can happen. So step out and have the courage to seek the life you were actually intended to live! You must also connect with the power of your voice, for the words you use are *crucial* for your success. They communicate your wants and needs and give you the ability to create an exciting future.

> **"You must leave your tribe to discover what's possible."**

Come out of your comfort zones, start living in uncertainty, and start taking lessons from inspiring instructors who will teach you how to present yourself to others in the most desirable and professional way. No one has ever been highly successful as an actor, singer, dancer, or performer without lots of first-rate training.

Develop a desire for excellence in your life. To do this, you must work hard and work smart. You must also go to places where people in your industry meet—seminars, workshops, panel discussions, screenings, Masterclasses, and showcases. Learn, connect, and just get out there!

Hide-and-seek is a game that should only be played when you are a child. As an adult, you need to work diligently to be found! And once found, you must be willing to show your authenticity, gifts, and vulnerability because that's the only way you can connect with others in a meaningful way. So, start seeking those who can help you grow, shine, and excel. It takes a team of supporters to have an amazing career. Only when you are *found* will your "real life" begin.

It's easy to hide, but it takes courage to be found! One of the biggest regrets people have at the end of their life is that they gave up trying to be found. Don't be someone who has never lived their true life!

"BE FOUND—NOW!"

*"I want to sing like the birds sing, not worrying what
I sound like or what others think." —Rumi*

CHAPTER 6

WHY ARE YOU HERE?

Some people enter showbusiness, sadly, for all the wrong reasons. They're unhappy and feel insignificant their whole life. So they enter this industry because they want to become "famous." This craving for attention, for being seen or heard, or for gaining importance makes them believe that this profession would be the best way to get the attention that they've been longing for. They didn't decide to embark on this path for the joy of learning the craft of acting! Now, if public adoration and fame are your reasons for entering the acting profession, it won't work! You need to quickly reevaluate these reasons. Only with a strong passion and commitment for the acting process and all that it entails will you be able to succeed in your goals.

Let me ask you a question. Would you win an Oscar for the way you live your life? The way you deal with your setbacks, disappointments, and problems? Think about it!

The more you become the best version of yourself, reacting to the difficulties you encounter along the way with optimism and fortitude, the greater the possibilities that await you for your life and career.

Your job is to interact with life at the highest emotional and passionate level and share this knowledge in your work. You need to be in loving relationships, be adventurous, curious, spend time with all types of people, and travel to places you are not familiar with. By experiencing a full life, you can bring unique, meaningful, and significant details to your acting. Start by living a "star-filled," quality life! This really works.

> *"The world is a book and if you do not travel you only read one page."* — attributed to St. Augustine

"How will I know when I'm a star?"

Well, you will know you're a star when everyone wants to be like you. When you enter a room, and you have a personality that people gravitate toward. They will also notice that when you have difficulties in your life, you seem to react to them differently than anyone else. You impress them with your reactions and your "nothing is going to stop me" attitude.

Think of a great movie star that you admire for their craft and their humanity. I want you to think for a moment that you are him/her. I want you to behave like that star, and react to your own problems as they would. Stars also had incredible obstacles and problems to overcome to enable the pursuit of their dreams. They have spoken about this at our Masterclasses around the globe many times. The difference is that they don't see them as problems but as opportunities to grow and strengthen their character, and as lessons to be learned so they can achieve their future greatness.

> *"To be an artist you must break barriers, shine a light into the darkness, and show people new possibilities."*

I have been fortunate to know and work with some very well-known and successful actors, singers, and performers from all over the world. I have noticed that they all have something in common. When they walk into a room, they spread a kind of positive "energy" everywhere. And I've also discovered that there are artists who can teach us all how to live an impactful and meaningful life. If you want to have a star-filled quality career, then show us by the way you live your life!

> *"If you want to achieve what you've never achieved, you have to become the person you have never been!"*

When you are a star in your own life, you bring this quality to the industry. So, be grateful, be positive, and be inspired to make the changes you need for your better tomorrow. Happy people transform more quickly into what they need to become to succeed.

> *"First, love the life you have, so you can have the life you want."*

CHAPTER 7

WHAT SPECIALNESS ARE YOU BRINGING TO SHOWBUSINESS?

What do *you* have to offer this industry that is truly special?

This happens to be the most important question that you need to answer before you begin this journey. Most people frankly have no idea what is truly unique or special about them. This is a big problem!

This industry isn't called Show-Up or Show-Off, it's called Show-*Business*! In business, you have to be very clear about what you are selling. What do you have to offer that audiences might want to buy? What value do you bring to this industry? I'm speaking about something that we currently don't have. (For a deeper understanding of this concept, read chapter eighteen: "You Are the Product!")

Well, the answer is always YOU. We don't have you. You are one of a kind. Let me be clear—I may not be speaking about the way you are right now. I'm speaking about a fully alive, charismatic, and powerful YOU. To achieve this, you need to awaken your soul, heart, and emotions by visiting museums; seeing theatre, opera, and ballet; reading inspirational books, great works of literature, and poetry; and watching foreign films. You need to be interested in the world around you and connect with everyone you meet. This will make you a more dynamic person. If you are not fully engaged in life, you are likely to be a person without any passion, energy, or emotions, and no one wants to pay to see someone like that perform.

We want to see the inspired, real you. You're authentic when you feel powerful, happy, open, and your soul is visible to others!

"Always have a positive effect on others around you."

You also need to know that at the beginning of your career, you will likely be hired for acting jobs based only on how you look and the specific type that you are. A lot of my students don't have a clear picture of who they truly are, and they need some professional advice on this important and extremely sensitive topic.

So, ask yourself, "What parts will I be asked to play based on my appearance?" If you look sexy or funny—can you comfortably and skillfully access those parts of yourself? Once you answer these questions, you then need to learn how to play these roles in your own unique way. There will never be anyone who can play a part the way you play it. Realize that you will need to learn techniques and methods on how to bring these attributes into your work.

You must be around coaches, friends, partners, and artists that encourage and support your unique qualities. Many great artists were often criticized or even ostracized when they first began because they were considered to be "too different." Sadly, this has stopped many incredible performers and actors that we will never know.

Most people want to be liked so desperately that they will never become their true selves. They're too afraid to be distinct from those around them. They refuse to stand out, and therein lies the real tragedy. If your main goal in life is to be liked by others, then you will never become authentic or happy, and your dreams will go unfulfilled. An exercise that I use with my actors and clients starts by asking them this question: "What qualities do you have that people would be interested in?" If they say, "Well, I'm charming, passionate, and funny," then I ask them to do a thirty-second video commercial where they show us those qualities. It's like a video you would make about yourself for a dating site, a potential job interview, or for an audition.

It's important that when you do this commercial, you highlight these qualities. Because if we don't see it, it's not there. We only believe what we see!

I also advise them to promote these appealing qualities everywhere they go, for you never know who you could encounter on your journey. If you want others to recognize your specialness, show it.

When you think of all the great stars, past or present, you remember them because they are unique. Above all, they weren't afraid to be their irreplaceable and unapologetic selves. Actors like James Dean, Sidney Poitier, Marilyn Monroe, Marlon Brando, and Robin Williams knew who they were, took risks, and showed us their magnificence. If you don't already know their work, you really need to! They are regarded as highly influential leaders in the acting profession and film industry. Lady Gaga, Jim Carrey, Meryl Streep, Viola Davis, and Robert De Niro also know who they are, never apologize for it, and show the world their brilliance. This is exactly who you need to become—the unapologetic, risk-taking, and completely vulnerable you.

> *"We don't need another actor who is like someone
> we already have." —Stanislavski*

We don't need another Brad Pitt. We already have him! What we don't have is YOU. Don't be a copy; nothing will ever be as good as the original. Your quirks, imperfections, behaviors—the ones that you may not like—are probably the very gifts that you will need to learn to embrace. You have to bring these qualities to the surface in order for your acting to soar. This will start you on your road to artistic freedom, which will bring you to your success!

Remember, show the world something they have never seen before: the truly authentic, open, and powerful YOU!

**"Unless you're ready to be distinct,
you're going to become extinct."**

CHAPTER 8

BECOME A "WORLD EXPERT"

*"You will only be extraordinary at a profession
that you love!"* —*Les Brown*

Some students are not exactly aware of what a great acting class should be like. So, here it is; a great class should be four things: inspiring, motivating, fun, and challenging.

Class must be so stimulating that you never want it to end. Classes that don't motivate, support, or push you beyond what you think is possible will never help you to improve or succeed. Finding the right class is not so easy to do, but you must never give up the search.

Sometimes the class is only as good as you are. If you are a pessimistic person, you will approach a class in a pessimistic way, but if you're an optimistic person, then the class will reflect this too. In fact, we don't see the world or anything the way it is; we only see it the way we are.

Throughout my career, I was fortunate enough to be in some wonderful classes, but I always felt something was missing from those classes. Since I didn't find what I was looking for, I ended up creating the class I always wanted to be in. This happened in the year 2000 when I was asked to teach a five-week Masterclass in Paris. I began working with French, Italian, Russian, Spanish, Israeli, German, Polish, Australian, Greek, and British actors. I've now worked with actors from seventy-five countries, and I've realized that students learn best by doing, not just by listening. So I continue to create new exercises and methods to make my classes more effective, powerful, and transformational.

"I prepare my actors for a future they cannot see."

*"The actor has to develop his body. The actor has to work
on his voice. But the most important thing the actor
has to work on is his mind." —Stella Adler*

She is so right!

I wanted to become a visionary teacher, someone who teaches for the actor's future needs. I know that audiences are always changing and expecting more from the actor. So I teach the actors to develop skills they will need for future employment, to prepare them for the show-business of tomorrow.

The most valuable reward for me is to see my actors succeed, by being fully prepared and ready for whatever the industry is asking of them. My techniques are designed to make actors fully available, confident, spontaneous, powerful, and emotionally alive. True artists keep developing these skills while collaborating and working on their projects.

"If you're not creating, you're just waiting!" —Kevin Pollak

Unfortunately, some of the students that come to my classes don't know how to learn. Our school experiences did not teach us the joys of learning, failing, and growing. All I ever want is for my actors to get the most out of my classes, seminars, or sessions by transforming their careers and lives beyond their goals and dreams. I find that the actors' biggest problem is that they are not being trained in the right order for them to learn, grow, and succeed.

Here is a list of how you should prepare for the class so you will have a successful experience! *First, make room in your mind to learn!* Old ideas must die for new concepts to be born.

1. When you're in the class, be prepared to give. Whatever you need for yourself, give this to others. Give things like passion, confidence, and energy. Share this, and you'll receive it back threefold.

2. Be ready to make big changes. Only through change will you discover your possibilities.

3. Successful people always want to know other people. So, connect with everyone, to create long-lasting artistic relationships. People love to work with friends and other like-minded colleagues on great projects.

4. With every exercise, get more committed and allow yourself to become more emotional. Emotional people are always more powerful. Find the excitement and the challenge in the exercises you are given. Learn to find the lesson, not the pain, in every situation, and use the constructive criticism you are given as a tool to grow and expand.

5. Put pressure on yourself. Like a pot on a stove, once you start to boil, that's when real transformation occurs.

> **"A person's true character and talent are revealed only under pressure."**

6. Become more open to expressing and connecting with your emotions. How emotionally available you are will determine the level of your acting success. (Read chapter thirty-three: "Transformational Exercises." This will help you connect with your emotional power.)

7. Be positive! Positive energy always attracts the right people into your life. A successful attitude attracts other successful people.

8. Bring love to the class! Love brings light to show you the way, whereas fear brings negativity and darkness—stopping everything. You will always be remembered for all the positivity and joy that you add to the class.

"Acting is not a way of life; acting is a way TO life!"

THE ACTOR'S CONTRACT

Make a strong commitment to your future! Once you have found the right class for you, I believe that both the teacher and the student should work in harmony together. So, I came up with a contract for my actors. If you genuinely want to learn what I or other teachers have to offer, follow the conditions of this contract. If you abide by them, both you and your teacher will succeed in this magical endeavor.

THE CONTRACT

A contract is an agreement between two parties clearly stating what is required from both sides.

1. I must be willing to find the "real" truth about myself. Most people have no idea who they "truly" are.

   "An unexamined life is not worth living." —Socrates

2. I understand that, in order to achieve my dreams, I must be willing to feel foolish and be uncomfortable. Anyone who has ever tried to do anything new feels like this.

3. When I perform, I must give more than anyone ever expected of me, including myself. You need to constantly prove to *yourself* that you are serious about your craft and your dream.

4. I acknowledge that I will meet people who will not see my gift. That is the most common thing in the world, but it must never stop you.

5. I will not judge my gift. I will let others do that for me. Your job is to give your gift to the world without judging it.

6. I am completely responsible for my career and myself. I accept where I am in my career, and only I can change it.

7. I will be easy to work with. You'd be surprised how many difficult people try to get into this business, and, of course, fail. So, be flexible and nice!

8. I will never complain or blame anyone. When you complain or blame others, you lose your power.

9. I will be open to new information and new possibilities. You must forget everything that you think you know to learn something new.

10. I will bring joy and passion to my craft every day. It's the fuel you need for success. Without joy and passion, your dream remains just an idea.

11. I will maintain an optimistic attitude no matter what happens.

12. I will learn to trust and believe in my artistic instincts. Don't question your instincts; they come from your heart, and your discerning heart is always right.

13. I understand that, to achieve any of this, I must first . . . FULLY WAKE UP! You may not know it, but trust me, YOU ARE SLEEPING. Wake up to all your possibilities!

Signature:

_____

NOTE: I know that I will have to remind myself of these rules daily.

Make a copy of this contract. Post it on your bathroom mirror or refrigerator to ensure you see it EVERY DAY!

YOU MUST PAY A PRICE TO ENTER THIS BUSINESS.

"The price you pay to live your dreams or pursue your goals is facing all your doubts and fears. The reward for such a courageous act is realizing that all your doubts and fears were just an illusion and that your dream was always REAL!"

CHAPTER 9

TALENT IS NOT ENOUGH!

"Having talent is not special. What's special is having the courage to see where your talent will take you!"

Every single person on this planet was born with some kind of special ability. Unfortunately, having talent in and of itself will not be enough to succeed in your desired field. What is special is the person who has the courage to invest in themselves and also learn how to promote and showcase their gifts to others. It's criminal that the vast majority of people never do anything with their gifts or potential. Our gifts are not something we just share between our close friends or family but something I believe the world needs.

"The graveyard is the richest place on earth because it is here that you will find all the hopes and dreams that were never fulfilled, the books that were never written, the songs that were never sung, the inventions that were never shared, the cures that were never discovered, all because someone was too afraid to take that first step." —Les Brown

Rob the graveyard of your passion, gifts, dreams, and ideas! Please don't get buried with all your treasure still inside you.

Here are ten practices that you must do regularly to keep your talent growing and thriving. If you don't, others will book the job you should have gotten! The most successful people I know are flourishing because they work more diligently and effectively than anyone else. They give that raw talent a workout every day, as this is the only way it's going to get stronger. You will need to change to increase your talent and attract more success. Habitually doing these practices will help you become a professional working actor.

1.   Exercise and take a dance, mime, fencing, pilates, or yoga class—whatever gets you in touch with your body. This is where all of your gifts, talents, and instincts live.

2.   Go to places where you can observe many people. Evaluate them as though you are going to write a book about them. Pay attention to their body language, their clothes, and their hairstyles. What is your instinct telling you about them?

3.   Take singing lessons. It doesn't matter how you sound, but whether you can access the power of your voice. The quality and control of your voice gives you the ability to persuade and command attention.

4.   Work on scenes, monologues, or exercises that take you out of your comfort zones. For example, dress up and play someone else for an afternoon. Use a completely different voice, physical gesture, mannerism—even an accent. I suggest playing someone who is the complete opposite of you. Convince the

world that this is who you are. Go out as this character. It's better to go with someone else, so you can encourage each other. Your performance should be so truthful that anyone you meet would think this is who you truly are.

5. Keep enhancing your five senses. Seeing, feeling, smelling, hearing, and tasting. Become more sensitive today than you were yesterday.

6. Read a different play or script every week with your friends. This creates an artistic community.

7. Express whatever is going on inside of you. Unexpressed sadness and anger will kill your career! Sit silently, and listen to the secrets your heart and body are telling you.

8. Watch great films—from the old classics to current ones. Actively seek experiences that bring joy, fun, and excitement into your life.

9. Spend time in nature and see life from a new perspective. Nature connects you to your soul.

10. Play an even bigger role in this world than you are right now. Devote your energy and talent to a charity, a cause, or an injustice. Always think, "What can I give?" Because the more you give, the more you get.

> ***"You're either getting better or bitter,***
> ***but no one ever stays the same!"***

CHAPTER 10

IT'S THE "WOW" FACTOR

The big change that is happening in showbusiness right now is that audiences, agents, directors, producers, casting directors, and the industry in general are no longer satisfied with just a very good or excellent performance. Now, when they meet and see you act, perform, sing, or dance, they want to be WOWED!

This is because we are now constantly bombarded and overwhelmed by amazing talent from all over the world. Through social media, we are now wowed by performances in a way that was never accessible to us before. Access to global talent is much more visible. So now your performances must be mind-blowing. You have to give them a performance that they wish they had filmed. This may sound crazy, but it's true. The "WOW" factor is now the expected norm.

Sometimes you will enter the audition room and the role you're auditioning for has just been cast. Alternatively, maybe the casting director feels—now looking at you—that you're not exactly the type they were looking for. The only way you're going to set yourself apart from the rest is if you are so talented and magnetic that they are willing to change the character's gender or ethnicity, or even write a different character altogether—so that you can be in their production. This has happened several times with many of my actors. You have to be that spectacular!

"Wow!" is an involuntary sound to an experience that is so surprising, profound, and emotional that you make this vocal reaction unintentionally.

Getting a "Wow!" sound out of people is not particularly easy. To attain this, you will have to leave your acting comfort zones and become a gold-medal Olympic actor. The best of the very best! You have to show us something we have never seen before.

Here are some of the behaviors and actions that will make people say "WOW!"

5 THINGS THAT WOW US!

1. Your performances go beyond everyone's expectations. They are full of unpredictability, nuance, and depth. You are so truthful and vulnerable that we no longer see you—we only see the character.

2. You strive to make artistic choices that no one else would dare to make. You bring your unique creativity to your work, and this allows us to see memorable performances.

3. You have the courage to show us your raw, spontaneous, imperfect self.

4. Your commitment to your dream, craft, or talent is never-ending. You need no motivation from others to move forward. You inspire people with your passion, artistry, creativity, and vision of tomorrow.

5. You train with the best teachers, coaches, or mentors, wherever they may be. Nothing is too much for you. You never tell anyone about your money or time constraints. You always grow bigger than your problems.

CHAPTER 11

HOW TO CREATE UNFORGETTABLE PERFORMANCES

"It's not about losing yourself in the role. It's about finding yourself in the role." —Uta Hagen

Before you start working and processing a scene or script you will be performing, read it *very slowly* so that you understand every word—including all the directions listed. You can read it silently but you *must* also read it *out loud.* Have a dictionary close by to look up the definitions of each word, as it may inform the meaning of what you are saying in a way you did not understand before and therefore provide you better insight into the performance. (I have found that most actors or singers don't fully comprehend what they are saying.) You will also need to understand what is truly being said beneath the words. (Please read chapter thirteen, "Words Are Never the Truth," for a greater explanation of this process.)

Understand that when a scene starts, it always starts in the middle, because something has happened before that has led you to the conflict in this moment. Now, the conflict in the scene is created when you have two strong needs that must be satisfied *by* the other person, but they are not interested in giving you what you need. You must know why the other person is so important to you. In fact, the other person *is* the reason you are speaking. Choose someone from your life who is so important to you that their presence makes you emotional, and for whom you're willing to risk becoming vulnerable to fulfill your needs.

THE FUNDAMENTAL NEEDS

You enter the scene with a hunger that needs to be fed—urgently. There is something very specific that you NEED the other person to DO (physically). For example, them giving you a kiss or hug, throwing themself on the floor, begging for forgiveness, crying, a *physical* action. The action you choose must be such that you see when they are doing it.

You also have something specific you NEED them to SAY (verbally) to you. Choose personal and affective words that would make you emotional. Emotional courage is what we want to see. For example, "I can't live another second without you," and "You are my destiny," or "Only when I'm with you am I truly alive." Know that being truthful is not enough. There must be an URGENT need to transform the other person. You have to understand why your wants and needs must be satisfied now.

For example, "Today, I will fully express myself, even though it's difficult for me. And for the first time ever, I will believe in myself enough to tell you my true desires."

Only when your needs are MEANINGFUL, EMOTIONAL, and URGENT will the scene become truly alive.

"Only when you make impactful and dynamic choices will an audience become fascinated watching you."

What you want the other person to do and say must be something difficult to acquire. The more problematic, the more interesting and dynamic the scene will be. You must also know when you have achieved these two goals. Once you have succeeded, the scene is over. If you're still talking, you haven't gotten all your needs met, or you haven't chosen a strong enough objective for the *entire* scene.

You must also discover **why** you need these things now, and then show us **why** this relationship is so important to you.

"There's a lot of detective work that needs to be done before great acting can occur."

You must place all your energy on getting a *reaction* from the other person, not focusing on how you need to feel. Consider it the "Interrogation Room" method. You are not there to make a statement. You're there to get a *reaction* out of the other person. Ben Kingsley says, "I don't like to act. I like to react."

Audiences respond when you NEED something extremely important from the other person! Always ask yourself, "What do I need from the other person that is so *life or death* important to me?" And when your needs are that important, you are no longer concerned with playing the emotion, and therefore the emotion will occur organically and in relation to what you are trying to achieve.

It's important that you choose primal needs for your scenes, such as LOVE, SEX, MONEY, POWER, and CONTROL, because everyone in the world can understand and connect with these human needs. People are willing to die for these things. Now, the more difficult it is for you to attain those needs, the better the scene.

Imagine you're running into an emergency room because someone you love is there. When you called the hospital earlier and asked what's going on, they wouldn't give you any information over the phone. So you arrive at the hospital and rush over to the doctor and ask, "Doctor? What's going on?" Now, you are trying to appear calm and collected, but underneath your heart is pounding. You're confused and terrified. This emotional, physical, and psychological state you're experiencing is ideal for acting. Uncertainty, fear, and loss of control—they all contribute to the gravity of the situation, making for the best scenes.

We have to see you struggling to overcome your inner and outer obstacles. Know that behavior and reactions speak louder than words. These elements are not easy to incorporate, but this is why acting is a learned craft. It takes dedicated work and time to perfect powerful performances!

"All scenes are like emergency moments played out calmly."

It's important to know the power of silence or of a "filled/pregnant" pause, which can be very effective in a scene because the silent subtext speaks louder than words. (The "Pinter Pause" was an important device used by the British playwright Harold Pinter.)

"Only speak if you can improve on the silence."

THE TECHNIQUES

THE WHY

"Why?" You must know internally why you need what you need now. Why are you doing what you are doing right now? Don't over-plan how you're going to do it. If we see your plans or fake or manufactured emotions, you will give a superficial performance. Nobody wants to see that.

Your WHY must be the burning need to take action. The WHY must engage your heart and gut, not the mind. When you have a strong WHY, the scene will play out spontaneously. Playing the *how* creates an uninteresting and flat performance. When you discover the urgent *why*, you can uncover the true motivating forces of the scene.

Knowing WHY is your gateway into the truth of the dialogue, the character, and the meaning of the scene.

THE RELATIONSHIP

One of the biggest problems actors face is that they are not clear about the relationship they are having with the other characters. Every scene is propelled from a specific RELATIONSHIP. *Always play the relationship needs, not the plot.* Once you discover and engage in a meaningful relationship, the scene becomes more profound, and everything starts to flow. To establish romantic chemistry, *share your charismatic personality with the other actor.*

THE STAKES

What do you risk losing? Make it as personal and meaningful to you as possible. When the stakes are very high, everything means something. Ask yourself, "How can I make the other person and situation more important to me?" So, every look, movement, word, and gesture has intense meaning. The higher the stakes, the more interested the audience will be in watching the scene. It must feel life-changing if you get what you need and devastating if you don't.

THE EVENT

You must figure out: "What's the event?" What is happening in the scene that has *never* happened before? Find the uniqueness of this moment, and we won't be able to look away. Make a list of the life-changing moments that have occurred in your life. An event is something that, after it happens, you are significantly transformed in some way—forever!

THE MOMENT RIGHT BEFORE

Where are you coming from? What's happened to you before you arrived at your location? The character has had a life up to this point, and therefore you can't just start from nothing. All scenes start from something that's happened before. You must come into every scene emotionally loaded with a *physical* and *verbal* need. Make sure you're fully prepared for this.

WHERE ARE YOU?

Where is this scene taking place? Pick a specific location. Different locations create different feelings. How long have you been there? This will affect your state of being. Pick a place that has an emotional meaning that would affect you. Maybe a location with complicated memories, where something significant occurred. Incorporate the specific feelings or senses that are triggered from that location into your work.

OBSTACLES—YOURS AND THEIRS

Know that when you enter the scene, the other person thinks and feels the total opposite of you. They absolutely do not want to give you what you need. That's your external obstacle. You have to convince them, in every way possible, to give you what you need. The greater the obstacle, the greater the performance.

An example of powerful internal obstacles that I like would be a feeling of being *lost* and *confused* while trying to figure out what to do or say as the scene progresses. You should feel as if you never know what to do or say. You also have two opposing thoughts that the character is thinking about at the same time. For example, someone says to you, "Do you want to go out with me?" You're thinking, *Yes!* And *No!* And at the very last moment, you choose one. When you're lost and unsure of how to answer, it creates interest, suspense, and tension in the scene.

Another powerful choice is *not being good at the task or role you are expected to play*. For example, a lawyer, doctor, detective, lover, therapist, or prostitute—any role you can think of—*you're just not good at it*. Now, you're trying to play these roles impressively on the outside, but what the audience doesn't know is that you're attempting to hide your incompetence with a strong layer of confidence. These inner struggles are captivating to watch. Without obstacles, the scene is not captivating.

Always ask yourself this very important question: "Where are my internal and external conflicts in the scene?" This is absolutely vital for any actor to know before starting any scene!

INSIDE-OUTSIDE ACTING

On the outside, you show one thing, but on the inside, you feel something completely different. Like a pressure cooker or a volcano, calm on the outside and boiling hot on the inside. The inside wants to express itself, but it doesn't. That's what people do every day in their lives! They learn to hide their true feelings, desires, and emotions. So our job is to behave like human beings, not like an actor.

INNER MONOLOGUE

Visualize what you're saying and feeling before you start to speak. Then visualize powerful images of what they are saying and how it's making you feel. Never stop thinking about the character's thoughts, and also react physically to everything you are visualizing. Your inner monologue allows us to be aware of your private thoughts—what you are truly feeling about this situation that is not being communicated by words.

> *"Always keep thinking, because the camera captures all your thoughts."*

PERSONALIZE

Personalize your objective, the person, and the scene. It's important that what occurs in the scene is something you can relate or connect to emotionally from your life. Also, you may choose a person from your own life to substitute for the other actor. I tell my actors to pick at least three people in their lives that affect them for good or bad and substitute them in their minds for the other actor. The more personal the scene is to you, the more of an impact it will have on *you* and others. You can also use Stanislavski's "as if" method of imagining. What if this similar situation actually happened to you? How would you feel; how would you respond? Now, if you can profoundly connect to the other actor, you don't have to substitute someone else for them; you can just be with them. That can create a very intense and electric performance because you completely trust one another and are lost in the moment with each other.

If your scene is based on a romantic relationship, one way to develop more connection is to reveal some of the biggest traumas, hurts, secrets, or beautiful moments you have had in your own life to your costar. Try it, if you feel comfortable doing so. Something that maybe no one knows or only your closest friends would know. If you share your heart and soul with each other, you become vulnerable and immediately share a special bond and connection. If you have to be in love with your costar, find something about them you could genuinely fall in love with—from their personality, their energy, or even an eyebrow. Pick something, and then endow it with a great deal of meaning for you. This method has worked for many of my actors. *Find a method that works best for you.* Use these or other tools to access and illuminate the truth of the scene and your character.

> ### "Acting is the most courageous and vulnerable profession in the world."

Also, choose clothing that helps you behave, move, and feel like the role you are playing. The perfect coat can strengthen the character. For example, the iconic fedora hat and whip from the *Indiana Jones* movies are an important part of the character. In several films, you'll notice that clothing becomes a crucial element of an actor's performance. Watch Viola Davis in *Ma Rainey's Black Bottom*. Her glossy, heavily applied, and almost tragic *emotional* makeup helps us connect with her vulnerability beneath her outer shell. In addition, her ostentatious clothing tells us so much about her struggles as an artist and as a black woman during the 1920s. Makeup and clothing are clearly an integral part of her performance. It's a must-see!

Choose props you can use in the scene that have meaning for you. Or figure out a way to make them meaningful. Watch Tom Hanks in *Cast Away*, acting opposite a volleyball named Wilson. When the volleyball floats away, the audience is moved to tears. When you personalize or endow your props, your scene will jump off the page.

ACTING IS *REACTING*

Before you speak, make sure you have a meaningful connection to *all the words* you are saying.

> *"Denzel Washington dissects every word and every thought that is possibly going on in the scene." —George C. Wolfe*

While you are speaking, have a physical and emotional reaction to what you are saying and a reaction to everything the other person says, does, or doesn't do.

Also, in every scene, there must be a *revelation*—something that is said or done that you did not expect—something that really shocks you or takes your breath away. Take your scene partner's behavior and dialogue extremely personally. It's important to remember that what your partner is saying is 25 percent true. This way, you are being affected by what they say. You only argue over something that is truthful, which you desperately don't want to be true.

> *"Listen with your blood." —Stella Adler*

If you're *just thinking* and not physically or emotionally *reacting* to what they are saying, you will seem disconnected from the scene. Also, find the trigger words in the scene—these are the words that affect you and set you off. The world-renowned acting coach Uta Hagen said, "What will help your reactions is to expect the other person to do and say the opposite of what they actually will do and say. You react strongly in life when someone says or does something you did not expect."

INSTINCTS

React with your instincts! Don't be logical when reacting because in a high-pressure moment, no one usually is. Instincts create accidental and unpredictable moments in a scene, and they are often remembered as the most powerful moments in film history. There are so many examples of this. When you're lost in the moment, your character's needs and instincts take over.

PROMOTE YOUR POINT OF VIEW

It's very important that you *promote* your character's point of view. Accept and understand what your character's needs are, how they behave, and what they believe in. You never judge your character because every person in the world always thinks their actions are "right" at the moment they are doing them. Justify and embrace your character's actions no matter what. This takes deep knowledge, understanding, and empathy for your character.

> *"Love your character so much that you would*
> *cry if they died." —Vadim Perelman*

Your job is to *promote* their point of view and actions in the most positive way possible. You must actually fall in love with your character's needs and wants. Even if the character is committing the most heinous of acts, they themselves do not think what they are doing is wrong. Do some research and then write a list of all the justified reasons why you are doing what you are doing. When you unearth your character's thoughts, feelings, motivations, and desires, you become attuned to *their* way of thinking and behaving.

HISTORY

Remember, you're playing a human being, not a caricature. For some roles, find the historical and societal connection to the character's behavior and mindset in the scene. Create a compelling backstory without choosing safe, simple, or average choices. Create the history for the other characters in your scene as well.

In the next chapter, you will find twenty-eight questions that will help you create a backstory/history of the character you are playing. When you understand everything that's happening in the scene and have a firm grasp of who the character is, then you can just BE this person. You don't have to ACT anymore. Audiences only want to see the real thing, which can only happen when you are in this state of BEING.

TACTICS

These are different ways in which you are trying to get what you need in a scene. What are your tactics? Are you using charm, sex, intellect, humor, guilt, sadness, or anger to achieve your goals? There are many approaches you could take. Play a few different tactics or scenarios in the scene, and you will discover which are the most effective ones. Are you a master manipulator, or do you blame others? Observe any teenager trying to borrow the car from his unresponsive parents and you will learn all you need to know about tactics! The more interesting the tactics, the more compelling your performance will be. Tactics must be constantly changing. Always try different ones.

ARC

What is your character's arc? You must start in one place, emotionally and physically, and end somewhere different. Perhaps you begin feeling tense, and then you become calmer in the scene. An arc is an emotional journey where you might begin nervously and then end confidently. To keep the scene interesting, you must flow from one emotion to another organically and seamlessly. Great performances always have powerful arcs.

ACTIVITY

You must physicalize what you're feeling in your body at all times. Actors must also be engaged in a physical activity. That's why they yell "Action!" on a movie set; they don't yell "And . . . speak!" What are you doing when this person enters your space? What would you be doing if this person didn't come into your space? Are you eating, drinking, working on your laptop, texting on your phone? Maybe you're exercising.

But *how* you are doing your activity reveals what you are really feeling.

WINNING

How is your character trying to win their objectives in the scene? We love watching winners, not victims. The actor with the strongest needs drives the scene and gets our attention. You are trying to achieve your goals, even under the most improbable of circumstances. Figure out how you're going to win!

> *"Remember, the actor that drives the scene forward is the one everyone watches."*

Acting is like an explosive tennis match. One actor hits the other with information that they think will win them the moment, but then the other actor absorbs this information, reacts, and hits back—interpreting the information to his advantage in order to win the next moment. The greatest scenes go back and forth energetically like a Wimbledon final. Remember, you are a professional team player. So, you need to work together and be on your best game to win. Dynamic actors feed off each other, which makes them both powerful! The audience is intrigued to see who will come out on top.

WORDS MISLEAD

As an actor, you need to fully comprehend and understand each word of what your character is truly saying. Many actors assume that what their characters are speaking is the truth. Know that for many reasons we can't always say what we mean and feel pressured to mislead or to be untruthful. The true meaning is always beneath the words. (Please read chapter thirteen, "Words Are Never the Truth," for a greater explanation of this process.)

LET IT ALL GO & SURPRISE YOURSELF

After you've done all your homework, you must let it go and trust your invested creative process to take you on the journey. Your technique must lead you to have a spontaneous life in the scene. Focus on the other person and show us your vulnerability, imperfections, and humanity. Once you have done all the work, you can unconsciously live, breathe, and make instinctive decisions as your character. This will be a bit different from your rehearsal because you're now living in this moment! Don't ever play the ending of the scene; we have come to see the entire journey that the character takes, not the ending. Know what you need, but never know exactly how you will achieve it—be open to freely change in the moment.

After doing all the research, preparation, and training, we should not see all the work you have done. The actor's job is to make the performance seem effortless. We should see you perceive, absorb, and react to everything you are seeing, feeling, and hearing at that moment—for the first time. Your energy and focus should be on the actions you must take to solve your character's crucial problems. Remember that behavior and thoughts are more powerful and interesting than words.

The great actor Anthony Hopkins said, "I read the script two hundred times until I know the text cold. Knowing it so well gives me a tremendous sense of ease and confidence."

"If we see you acting, you're doing it all wrong."

CHAPTER 12

THE RIGHT QUESTIONS CREATE SPECTACULAR ARTISTS!

"Dynamic choices make dynamic performances!"

I want you to know that people are dying to see THE TRUTH. There are so many overacted and untruthful performances in the world, which have led to the creation of a huge industry called Reality TV! Audiences would rather watch six "real" non-actors living in a house than a scripted television show or movie. Reality TV is a reaction to audiences yearning for more truth, which dominates the airwaves. It's the actor's responsibility to bring more genuine reality into their work in order to attract back the audiences.

"An unforgettable performance transforms the viewer and the actor."

I give my actors a set of questions to work through, and I tell them not to perform until they have answered all of these questions. Through focused practice, these questions will help you connect to the fifth level of truth—which you will read about in the next chapter. The more creative and insightful you are in answering these questions, the more extraordinary your performance will be.

Answer each question carefully and take your time. Only you will see these answers, so be truthful. This will certainly change your acting for the better, and maybe your life.

First, whenever possible, answer these questions about yourself—personally, for greater insight into yourself. If you don't know who *you* truly are, how are you going to connect with and understand a character you're supposed to portray? When you're out of touch, you will give a superficial and disconnected performance.

Second, ask the same questions about the character you are playing. The answers for the character should be complicated and complex. Create them by using your heart, instinct, and imagination rather than your rational brain.

"Talent is in the choices you make." —*Stella Adler*

28 PREPARATION QUESTIONS

1. What is your character's last name? Come up with a meaningful and powerful last name that has gravitas!

2. What are the details of your character's parents? What are their first names? What do they do? How do you feel about them? Did they love you? Did you love them? How did you have to behave to be loved by them? What was your overall relationship with them?

3. What kind of childhood did you have? What were the important lessons that you learned when you were young? What were three of the best and worst incidents from your childhood? What unresolved issues do you still carry with you from your childhood?

4. What drives and motivates your character? Do you have an understanding and emotional connection to everything you are saying? Have your choices made you vulnerable? What is the emotional objective in the scene?

5. Where did you just come from, before the scene starts? Where are you planning to go after this?

6. Why are you saying this or acting in this way—right now? What's the urgency?

7. Why does this scene exist? What is it trying to show you about your character's journey?

8. What could you lose in the scene? How can you make the loss affect you *personally*?

9. What makes you laugh or cry? What makes you happy, scared, or angry? What turns you on?

10. When were you first in love? What did you learn about this experience?

11. What is the *fear, loss, desire,* or *pain* that *initiates* your scene? Is it the fear of losing love, sex, money, power, or control? What are your character's fears and doubts? Where did they originate from? What are yours?

12. What are your NEEDS in the scene? What exact words do you need to hear from your partner, and what physical actions do you need them to do? (This is the heart and soul of any great scene.)

13. Can you visualize what you and the other character are saying so it emotionally affects you?

14. What are your physical activities in your scene? Physicalize your feelings in your body at all times. Your body language must be able to tell your feelings and the story without words.

15. If your character were an animal, what would it be? What animal are you in your life?

16. What is the meaningful relationship to the other characters in your scene? What is their history?

17. Where is the *conflict* in your scene? Can you make the stakes even higher?

18. What tactics are you going to use to get what you want? Will you use seduction, humor, manipulation, or love? Find your appropriate action words. "I want to manipulate, disarm, inspire, shame, seduce, frighten," and so on . . . so you can succeed and win the scene. What are the tactics that you use in your life?

19. What life-changing events shaped your character's life as an adult? What were the painful moments they experienced? How did that affect them? What were yours?

20. Where and when was your first sexual experience? How was it? What does sex mean to you? How do you use it?

21. What are you addicted to? Is it money, sadness, drugs, fame, pain, sex, or work?

22. What is it about your body that you like? What don't you like?

23. What is the best part of your personality? (Funny, honest, charming, etc.)

24. What is the worst part of your personality? (Impatient, pessimistic, perfectionist, etc.)

25. What part of yourself do you hide from others? What ideas, feelings, or actions have you taken that you are afraid to share?

26.   How would your character and you want to be remembered?

27.   Where in your life can you personally identify with the events and the character's needs? If necessary, create an imaginary circumstance that has the same emotional connection for you—use an "as if": *as if* that particular circumstance is happening to you. If you cannot connect with the event, what is a similar emotion that is being experienced that you can connect to?

28.   What are your physical and emotional preparations before you start the scene? You must come into the scene emotionally "loaded."

NOTE: The answers to these questions are only valuable if you can put them into your body and soul.

Identify, connect, and emotionally comprehend the event that your character is experiencing. Otherwise, there won't be any truth or vulnerability in your performance. Be honest, personal, and as specific as possible. It's well advised to do *research* to understand the mindset, actions, and behavior of your character. The choices you make will determine the kind of performance and long-term career you will have.

IN SUMMARY

Only when you know your character inside and out can you just BE.

"BEING" is what acting is all about!

CHAPTER 13

WORDS ARE NEVER THE TRUTH

As an actor, understanding the truth of what you're saying and doing is the most powerful weapon in your arsenal. Finding the real truth is tricky. A common mistake many actors make, when given a script, is that they assume that what they're saying is the entire truth, but the words are *never* the whole truth.

In everyday life, we rarely ever tell the whole truth. In life-changing moments— such as romantic occasions, breakups, important business deals, divorce, and so many others—how you honestly feel is masked by untruthful words. Words are always hiding the full truth. Find the true meaning in your lines. For example, "I never want to see you again!" could mean "I can't live without you." Now, you might be saying it as a test to see if the person you're in love with will walk away. In fact, we test people all the time with our words.

Your job as an actor is to find out what the character authentically means and also to bring something unique to the part you're playing.

You do this by finding out what they are truly feeling and discovering what they are emotionally going through. I'll say it again . . .

"Never play the scene that was written. Always play the scene the writer should have written—but didn't write."

People under pressure have trouble expressing how they feel in words. Life can be very complicated. It's because people are not articulate enough to use the right words when expressing their emotions. Most people aren't in touch with their feelings at all. In life, we rarely use the right words, for we lack the bravery to make ourselves vulnerable to others. In a scene, sometimes you're not speaking the truth at all.

I would say that the script is only about 25 percent of the truth. Sometimes more and sometimes less. You'll need to determine the remaining 75 percent for yourself. You can only do this by knowing a lot about life and understanding human interactions and intentions. Words themselves have no meaning. Words are only symbols until you give them significance. It all depends on which definitions you give them.

Let's take a word like *love*. Love is a powerful word, and if you look it up in the dictionary, there are many different definitions. You can tell someone "I love you," but they will have to decide which type of love you specifically mean. Are you talking about friendship, family, romantic, or forbidden love? There are so many! Maybe you meant *lust*. Did you use the wrong word? Did you mean *like* instead of *love*? Maybe you're not in love at all, but you're using this word to manipulate someone's feelings.

These are the questions you have to ask yourself. The process of figuring this out for a scene will add depth and richness to your underlying work. A great coach can help you unravel this. You may have a couple arguing and screaming about how much they hate each other in a scene. You may think that the scene is about an ugly breakup when in fact it's about two people trying to stay together. They're both fighting for love. "If you loved me, you would understand what I'm feeling—why I'm upset and what I'm needing from you." If they seriously hated each other, they would just leave. *You only argue with people you love and for the things you want the other person to care about.*

Here's an acting secret. You're always fighting for something that's missing in the scene, and that something is LOVE. Ask yourself, "Where is the love in the scene?" Everyone in life wants and needs to be loved.

"A great actor understands his character's thoughts, needs, and wants better than anyone watching!"

Read a wide range of books, and watch shows on psychology, sociology, anthropology, love, sex, passion, fears, and life, which explore different types of human actions and behaviors. Most importantly, be aware of *why* people do the things that they do. Also, know that if we told people the whole truth about everything we felt all the time, we would lose everyone we cared about. In life, we have to figure out how to express ourselves while still maintaining good relationships. Everybody has to do that!

THE FIFTH LEVEL OF TRUTH

One of the things that I teach my actors is something I call the *fifth level of truth*. Once you arrive at that fifth level, you have found the *real* truth concealed in the dialogue you are saying. You must be an investigator to understand the motivations behind the words of any scene you are in. You do this by first finding the "Why." The "Why" is the magic key that will open the pathway to finding the real truth. For example, ask yourself, "Why do I like making love?" Many answers can come your way, but the fifth level of truth will be your most honest. It is the fifth answer that you bring to the scene. So, to get to that truth, you must ask yourself "Why?" at least five times.

Most people will say they like to make love because it "feels good."

Then I ask, "Why does it feel good?"

"It feels good because it makes me feel free."

"Okay, but why do you want to feel free?"

"Because it makes me feel open and connected to another person."

"Why do you want to feel open and connected to someone?"

"Because it makes me feel loved."

"All right, but why do you want to feel loved?"

(Now we come to the real truth, the answer to why *everyone* in the world likes making love.)

"Because it makes me feel alive." That's the fifth level of truth!

Most people only know the first two levels, but as an actor, you must know the true meaning behind every action, reaction, and behavior that you have in life. This practice will give you a greater insight into life, and you will be able to bring this knowledge to your character's needs and wants. The first four answers to your "Why" are about 20 percent of the truth, but the fifth answer takes it all the way up to 100 percent.

The deeper the search for truth, the more powerful an artist you will become. Your job is to understand the whole truth for all the characters in the scene. You may play a character that's dating a different person every night, and you may think that this person must be very happy and free. However, when you get to that fifth level, you come to realize that he or she might be doing this because they feel worthless and empty inside. This is their way of "connecting" with someone who makes them feel alive momentarily. The fifth level of truth will bring your character's motivations and desires to the surface, making the scene much more compelling. *Find the fifth level of truth before you perform any part.*

Imagine you are playing a detective trying to interrogate a murder suspect. What does the detective want? The first level of truth is to solve the case. This will make for a one-note and very bland performance.

So, let's investigate the scene further. The better choice will come from finding a deeper truth, therefore increasing the stakes. For example, if the detective doesn't get the suspect to confess, he will be fired and won't be able to support his wife and kids. Then he will feel like a failure and less of a human being. He feels scared for the first time in his life by the one criminal that he can't seem to break or understand.

Additionally, he wants to solve his case because he wants his life and career to have meaning and purpose. These are all deeper truths than what's on the page. The more you uncover, the greater and richer your performance will be.

Here are some more truths.

THE EMOTIONAL TRUTH

We are primal and emotional human beings. Feelings are like a running river. The way you feel about anything or anyone constantly keeps changing. It gets more intense or less intense, but it always keeps moving. You need to find the *emotional river* of your character. Focus on what you desperately need and want. It must be something powerful that will force you to take *risks* in your scenes, and if the stakes and the danger are high enough, audiences will be anxious to watch it. Remember, be emotionally connected to every word you're saying.

THE PHYSICAL TRUTH

A great deal of human communication is nonverbal. Expressing yourself with words can be complicated and even misleading. This is why physical and visual contact is important in trying to understand what someone is truly saying. Know that 85 percent of acting happens when you're not speaking but reacting. When someone is talking, you're watching their eyes and body language to see if they mean what they are saying. The body never lies, and the eyes are the windows to the soul. Don't just listen to someone's words. The great actor Laurence Olivier said, "Watch their legs to see if they are speaking the truth because watching all the parts of the body can tell you if they are being truthful in what they are saying."

The more you discover the real truth about yourself and your life, the more you will know the truth about someone else. This clarity, once mastered, can bring powerful new insight and knowledge to your work.

Great acting, like life, is complicated and messy. The accomplished actors whom I have known spend a significant amount of time trying to find out everything they can about the characters they play. This goes beyond just the details in the script. They give performances that no one ever expects. Samuel L. Jackson says, "Your character should be so interesting that when you leave the screen, the audience should want to follow you." That's a powerful concept! Watch some of Sam's films, and you will see unique, interesting, and very memorable performances that make you want to know what happens to him when he is no longer *on* the screen. He is a consummate actor!

Your character has lived a whole life prior to the events described in the script. You must know as much as you can about your character's past so that you can deal with the present. If you don't understand your character's past history, you'll be lost. Imagine not knowing where you came from. If you don't know your past, then you have what I call the "Actor's Amnesia," and this will obliterate any authenticity that you must have in every scene you're in.

So, you need to understand everything about the character—how they think, what they like and dislike, what their life is about up until this present moment. What are their dreams, joys, secrets, fears, disappointments, and desires? Take all that knowledge and insight and bring it to this moment. It's *not* something you have to show; it's something you have to embody. Know it in your heart, soul, and gut, and then you'll give an *unforgettable* performance!

> **"Comprehending the complexities of human relationships and understanding different ways we communicate with one another is what separates professional artists from amateur actors."**

CHAPTER 14

DARE TO BE DIFFERENT!

One of the strongest ways to become successful in showbusiness is by being willing to show your uniqueness and your innate differences. An actor demonstrates his talent in his performances and at auditions. Actors have to present themselves in front of casting directors, producers, directors, and network executives to get a job.

To become an unforgettable performer, you have to ask yourself, "How would everyone else play this part?" This is what I call the *universal choice*. Then you need to figure out how you're going to make a fundamentally *different* choice. An experienced coach can help you with this. (Read chapter three, "The Difference Between an Actor & an Artist," for more insight into this process.)

For smaller roles, you may not be able to play the role differently—you will have to give them exactly what they're expecting—but, if possible, do something a bit different. You do this by seeing the character and the situation in a uniquely different way.

Know that many prominent actors got their first big break in their career when they played contrary to the expectations of the role. Sharon Stone was no exception. She once told me the story of her audition for her big breakthrough film, *Basic Instinct*. Now, when you think of the character—she played a seductress, a murderer—you'd think this was a drama, right?

Well, Sharon's acting teacher thought it was a comedy. Seriously! Go on YouTube and see her screen test for this movie. Her acting coach, the late Roy London, thought it was a comedy, and that's how they prepared for it.

Throughout this entire audition, they're accusing her of murder and she's smiling, laughing, and flirting. This is what made her audition so remarkable. She told me that she heard lots of actresses in the audition room yelling and screaming and playing it as an intense drama. She decided to keep it light. Her unique choice to "go against the grain" inevitably got her the role.

When you think of unforgettable roles, such as Hannibal Lecter in *The Silence of the Lambs*, how would most actors play this role? Remember, he eats people. But what Anthony Hopkins did was he played it with great charm, sophistication, high intelligence, and a bone-chilling calmness within him. He was completely still, and that paradoxical choice was frightening to watch.

When an audience sees a character, they have expectations on how this character should behave, but once you play it differently from what they expect, you command their attention. Tennessee Williams said that Marlon Brando did not play the character he wrote in *A Streetcar Named Desire*. He wrote someone who is less human and less vulnerable, but what Marlon brought to the part of Stanley was something totally different. It was animalistic, magnetic, and dangerously unpredictable. If you have not yet seen this movie, you must!

Another extraordinary example of Marlon Brando's brilliance is from *On the Waterfront*. Brando is reacting throughout the entire movie in completely surprising ways. In particular, pay attention to the legendary taxi scene. For me, it's one of the most outstanding acting scenes ever filmed. When I last watched it, it made me cry because I was watching an acting genius. There are so many spectacular actors, but for me, Marlon Brando was the greatest of them all! Brando's acting style at the time was revolutionary, unique, and compelling. As Terry Malloy, he showed us his humanity full of vulnerability and imperfection, and he let us experience his pain and the dilemmas of being a longshoreman struggling to do the right thing. He won an Oscar for playing this role. His ability to convey such truthful organic emotions and passion was unparalleled. People had never seen anything like this before. Please see Marlon Brando's early films and you'll know what I'm talking about. An interviewer asked Stella Adler, "You taught Marlon Brando to act?" And she said, "No, I just showed him the door to acting, and he kicked that door down."

> *"Marlon had a revolutionary sense of truth. There's never going to be a better actor than Brando." —Sean Penn*

Another of my favorite performances that every actor must see is Lee J. Cobb in *Death of a Salesman*. The great writer Arthur Miller said that "Lee took my creation further out on the shore than I thought was possible. He was unafraid to enter the darkest corners of Willy's heart." Fortunately, the play version was filmed for television, and when you see it, you will know what I'm talking about. Lee originated the role on

Broadway, and no one has ever surpassed his performance. The better choices you make, the more talented you will be perceived to be. Playing a part differently, with dynamic choices, could change your career forever! Going against the universal choice has served my actors well, including when I coached Cameron Diaz for her first film audition in *The Mask*, with Jim Carrey.

> *"Never be afraid of the author. The actor's a*
> *free artist." —Anton Chekhov*

CHAPTER 15

SUCCEEDING AT AUDITIONS

For many actors, auditioning is the most feared and dreaded part of being in this business. Well, let me tell you that you must immediately change your mindset in regard to auditioning. If you dislike or hate auditions, you will not work. You must be willing to embrace and appreciate the certainty and uncertainty of the process.

What are the benefits of auditioning? Well, you meet other actors and show the casting director what kind of talented human being you are. You could also book a role of a lifetime! The positives are much greater than any negatives. An audition is a way for you to share your love of your acting process with others.

When my daughter Dora was seven years old, her teacher at school asked her, "What does your father do for a living?" She didn't say I was an actor; she said that I was an *auditioner* because when I was about to leave the house, she would ask me, "Dad, where are you going?" And I would always say, "I'm going to an audition." You know what? She was right. That is what I do for a living. I'm a professional AUDITIONER!

Auditioning is your JOB. Performing on set—well, that's like a VACATION.

Below is some very important advice to excel at your auditions. There are also a lot of self-tapes being requested from actors these days, and you must adapt to that process as well. (Read chapter eleven, "How to Create Unforgettable Performances," to prepare for an audition.)

Leading up to the audition, visualize things going extremely well. In your mind, see them loving you.

Don't sit before you enter the audition room. Energy drains away when you sit. Stand up and move around to get your body energized to wow them. Your body needs to tell the story just as much as your voice. Breathe and allow the energy to flow through you effortlessly.

1.   Develop the mindset that an audition is your opportunity to perform. You're not there to get the job. You're going in for the role you already have. Play the scene as though you're going on set to shoot it. All auditions are really *performances* and an opportunity to start a new relationship with people in the industry. You are there to give, not to get.

> **"You have not come to impress anyone—you've come to have a truthful, emotional, and physical experience in the scene!"**

2. Be thoroughly prepared and come in loaded for the scene. Focus on your needs and on getting a response from the other person. Be open, available, and flexible. In a way, you need to forget what you've been practicing. Be fresh, find all the moments, and connect with your instincts. Treat your auditions like a game of chess. There is never just one move to make; there are several. You already have the structure. So, feel free to discover and explore. Know *why you need what you need* when you start the scene, but don't be attached to *how* you're going to get it. When you don't know what you're going to do, that uncertainty keeps us watching.

3. When you enter the room, be kind to everyone. Remember, the pressure is on the casting director and their team to find someone for the role, not you. Go into the room to solve their problem. Know that everyone in that room is hoping you're the one! They're also not just looking for "great actors." They're watching your humanity to see if you're someone they can work and spend time with.

4. Don't come into the room with any of your personal negative issues like sadness, anxiety, or a chip on your shoulder. Don't make any excuses for having just gotten the script or that you didn't sleep very well last night. No excuses and no complaining! Just be present for your amazing opportunities, and SHINE!

5. Know your character. I suggest being this character from the moment you leave your house to the moment you finish the audition. Start to think like them and respond like them, and

when you walk into the audition room, show them a bit of the flavor of the character you are playing.

6. *Show us the part of yourself that is the character*. We want to see you being a real human being, not an "actor." Once you access this part of yourself, it is your responsibility to show us your imperfections and struggles. This is what makes you more human to the audience.

"Your imperfection is perfection."

7. Before you start, take a deep breath, and *let the scene take you*. Get out of your head and get into your body. Physicalize what you're feeling at that moment. Let your instincts take over, and make sure to *react to everything* the other person is saying or not saying. Great acting moments also happen when you're not saying anything. Thinking about and seeing images that your character is experiencing and feeling is crucial.

"Acting actually happens when you're not speaking." —Jessica Chastain

8. Make the reader or the casting director look good. You do that by being connected to them and taking their direction. Everyone should feel better now that you've arrived.

9. If you're very nervous, make the choice that the character is nervous, not you. Use this rush of adrenaline purposefully in your scene. Also, put your focus on the other actor,

and demand that they satisfy your emotional and physical needs right now! Remember, you're always speaking to get a reaction—physical and verbal.

10. Conduct yourself like an actor you truly admire and have the same confidence in your audition as they would. When you finish, leave successfully no matter what. Believe in yourself—even through the mistakes. Do everything at that moment as if you intended it to happen. Sean Connery played the first James Bond, and at the audition, the producer said, "It was only after we saw Sean walking confidently out of the audition room that we were convinced that he was the right person for the role." Every moment counts—including your departure!

Try reacting more strongly to the reader and make the event even more important. Even if the person reading the scene is not connecting to you, use that as an obstacle to conquer. If your performances don't change a bit every time you perform, the scene will become stale, and you certainly don't want that. The luxury of getting into the audition room is to experience the heightened energy and connect with the creative team.

The benefit of sending a self-tape is that you have time to do multiple takes. To explore the needs of the scene, use your creativity to make dynamic choices before choosing which take better suits the project. I recommend you work with a professional coach. The most significant mistake an actor can ever make is being afraid to make one. Love the auditioning process because you are only great at the things you LOVE.

"Your fears will stop when you make the other person more important and more interesting in the scene than you."

NOTE: Because the industry is changing, there are more and more self-tape auditions occurring. Make sure that every take you shoot is more meaningful than the previous take and performed from a *slightly* different perspective. Provoke a reaction from your reader, and listen more intently so you can physically and emotionally react more deeply. Also, be careful not to *over* shoot the audition, as the spontaneity can dissipate and it can quickly become mechanical and stale. When you feel you got it—you got it!

CHAPTER 16

UNBLOCK YOUR AUTHENTICITY

*"It is better to be hated for who you are than loved
for who you are not." —André Gide*

If you are afraid to be the REAL, AUTHENTIC YOU, know that this is the main reason your life and career are not moving forward. You have blocks that are stopping you from becoming your authentic self. Until you deal with those blocks, you won't become the actor, singer, performer, entrepreneur, or person that you must be in order to be truly successful and live your purpose. Your life's possibilities start once you are AUTHENTIC!

THE AUTHENTICITY KILLERS!

PEOPLE PLEASERS

This is the ultimate killer of your authenticity. Now, there's a difference between those who are people pleasers and those who just like to please people. There's nothing wrong with pleasing people, making them feel good by your humor, energy, or positivity, but if you don't wholeheartedly want to do those things, that's people pleasing. In the end, this will make you angry, bitter, and sad.

The reason you are doing this is you mistakenly believe it's the only way you are going to be loved. When you're a people pleaser, you always neglect your needs to make the other person's wants and desires more important than your own. You are hoping the other person will notice this and love you more, but, of course, that will not happen. Changing yourself for others just makes you more invisible. You end up feeling lonely, in pain, and resentful rather than receiving the love you are so desperately longing for.

LIVING IN THE PAST OR THE FUTURE

You're too afraid to change because you live in fear, and so you trust the past more than your future. You think by changing you will lose everything you've built for yourself, which is totally not true. Resistance to change always causes failure and unhappiness.

If you are stuck with the pain of your past or living in the fear of your future, you will never connect to your inner power. Only when you are living in the present are you able to pursue all your opportunities.

CONTROLLING PERSONALITY

If you have a controlling personality, you want things done exactly your way, and you are not willing to compromise or surrender to any other way—making yourself difficult to teach or work with. If you are unwilling to be flexible, you'll fail—every time. Controlling personalities don't allow anyone or anything in, and, as a result, you block yourself from having an amazing life.

Now, the opposite of control is surrender, and only when you surrender will you open yourself up to miracles. You will need a lot of miracles to succeed in this business.

> *"Miracles provide you with unimaginable opportunities, which bring you closer to your goals and dreams."*

I would like to tell you that miracles are occurring all around you right now, but to be able to benefit and recognize all the amazing miracles that are meant for you, you first have to believe with your heart and soul in three things: YOURSELF, your TALENT, and your FUTURE. Once you accept and affirm these ideas, miracles will continuously come your way.

NEEDING TO BE LOVED—NO MATTER THE COST

When you're willing to give up too much of yourself to be loved and accepted by others, you deny who you truly are. Some people are so desperate for love that they give themselves completely to others. Of course, you need to give a part of your heart away to be loved, but when you give it *all* away—you are left with nothing.

"Never ask people to give you what
you wouldn't give to yourself."

LOOKING FOR APPROVAL IN ALL THE WRONG PLACES

There are certain societies and cultures where one is told to always seek the advice and approval of others before taking any direct action. When you do this, you start to feel that everyone seems to know more about what's *best for you* than you do. That's ridiculous!

You have to believe in your own choices if you ever want to succeed in this or any other business. There are certain moments in life where no one can tell you what to do. You need to trust yourself and ask your own discerning heart for advice, not someone else's. Only take advice from those who have *visibly achieved* what you desire.

BEING A PERFECTIONIST

Perfectionism is not about self-improvement. Perfectionism is the belief that if we live and act *perfectly*, we can avoid pain and the judgment of others. Perfectionism is, at its core, about trying to earn the approval and acceptance of others. A perfectionistic person is someone who was raised being praised for their achievements, behavior, and performance. You must let go of those ideas to be able to find your true self. Perfection will prevent you from taking risks and showing your humanity, which is what makes you unique and special. There is nothing wrong with trying to be *exceptional*, but "perfect" does not exist. Striving for it will prevent you from making the mistakes that are necessary to become *extraordinary.*

NOT HAVING THE COURAGE TO LIVE YOUR LIFE

In French, the word *coeur* means "heart." You must be very connected to your heart in order to live the life you were meant to live. When you pursue your dreams, you will live in uncertainty and vulnerability. You must be willing to accept this state of being. Know that it also takes courage to be happy and believe in your dreams.

There is no place called "security." Be brave and live the life that you desire and truly deserve.

Psychiatrists who study the learning process have said that every one of us goes through four stages of learning to become a professional. Identify from the list below which stage you are at on *your* journey.

Stage 1: Unconscious Incompetence
At this level, you are not aware of how disconnected, unskilled, and unprepared you are for this journey. Everyone who enters showbusiness enters with blocks, fears, and doubts about themselves that they need to overcome. Don't worry. We all start like this!

Stage 2: Conscious Incompetence
At this stage, you become fully aware of what your professional and personal limitations are, but you are not sure how to conquer them. There will be moments when you feel that you will never be able to prevail over all of these obstacles. Know that this is all part of your growing

process. Everyone goes through this. The techniques and exercises in this book will help you overcome them.

Stage 3: Conscious Competence

You reach this level only after receiving extensive high-quality training and gaining awareness of what you have to do to perform at the top level successfully. However, it has not yet become second nature to you. If you don't consciously think about it, it won't happen. For example, it's like your first time driving a car. You have to be fully conscious of what you're doing in order to reach your destination safely.

Stage 4: Unconscious Competence

At this stage, you are performing at the highest level of your craft without worrying or thinking at all. It has become second nature to you because you have mastered the *techniques* of your art, craft, or skill. You are operating from instinct and heart, which is now flowing through you. At this final level, you are experiencing the joy and freedom of being the top professional you always dreamt of being. Congratulations!

> *"If I don't practice one day, I know it; two days, the critics know it; three days, the public knows it." —Jascha Heifetz*

CHAPTER 17

EMBRACE WHO YOU TRULY ARE

"The formula of happiness and success is just being actually yourself, in the most vivid possible way you can." —Meryl Streep

If people always think of you as being different, odd, a dreamer, and not following the crowd, chances are you are a creative person in some way. Sometimes, you will be admired for being different, but often you will be put down, made fun of, or heavily criticized. Either you gather your strength and are proud that you were born different, or you try to be exactly like everyone else. Well, most of society unfortunately chooses the second option. It just seems easier to fit in and act out a role that others have defined for you, which in the end buries your true nature, talents, and life!

You must not listen to the limiting group mentality taught to you by your family, friends, teachers, culture, and society. Please see the greater possibility that is calling out to you. Keep in mind that all the great artists, actors, musicians, performers, scientists, and inventors were thought of as being odd, strange, and different. It takes a unique person to get to the moon, be a music icon, become a global movie star, or create personal computers. They live in a world full of possibilities, magic, and wonder.

Soon after you were born, many of you were bombarded with negative messages about who you are, the way you behave, and the way you express your thoughts and feelings. Some of you were disapprovingly asked, "What's wrong with you? Why can't you be like everybody else?" Or, "What makes you think you're so special?"

Slowly but surely, you started to disconnect from your authentic self and began developing a fake self that seemed to be more acceptable to others. Most people lose their authentic selves around the age of four or five because they were told they had to behave in a certain way to be loved and appreciated. You've probably heard the phrase "Kids should be seen and not heard."

This form of criticism first comes from parents or caretakers and then from friends, teachers, and society. So, you start to think that what you are doing and feeling must be wrong. We've been taught to be ashamed and disregard our thoughts, needs, ideas, instincts, dreams, and goals.

Now, how do you know if you're faking your way through life? Well, you're ignoring your painful past traumas. You're mainly unhappy, you feel worthless, and you don't listen to your intuition. You feel like something is missing in your life, which there is—it's YOU!

It is so easy to get lost in this crazy world, and I see this when I teach actors, performers, and opera singers to be authentic onstage or on-screen. In the beginning, they have no idea what this fundamentally means. When you spend time living your *fake self*, you've accepted that you will be unhappy, and life will feel empty as you live the lie you've fallen prisoner to. By continually empowering the "fake self," you disconnect from the core of who you truly are. You become controlling and start to live in your head. When you live in your head, you become negative and limit your hopes and dreams. You then feel isolated, sad, and no longer in touch with your identity. You become a divided human being, battling with your true self, which will never come to fruition.

> *"He who cannot reveal himself cannot love, and he who cannot love is the most unhappy man of all."* —Søren Kierkegaard

Sadly, some will never escape the confines of their family, friends, culture, or past. To be a successful person, you have to escape from your *coma of comfort* and join a minority group of authentic individuals that have the courage to be who they essentially are—no matter the cost. These are the people that move cultures, industries, mountains, and societies forward.

Leonardo DiCaprio once told me that he only started to work seriously as an actor the moment he was willing to show casting directors and producers his authentic self. He decided not to worry what anyone else thought about him. He is one of the most respected actors working in Hollywood today because he continues to put his authentic self into his performances.

For you to reconnect, you will have to confront, acknowledge, and change the things that you have been unwilling to face before. Many of these things you may not even be consciously aware of, and you will need an accomplished mentor to help you because no one is able to see their own blocks. It's just not possible.

"You are like an orchestra. You must first discover different parts of yourself so you can be in harmony."

Have the courage to move toward a productive change. This is serious work that must be done and done quickly. You will have to discover your true self by going past the limited view of who you think you are.

If you commit to your true self, you will discover that the things you've been told were *wrong* about you are actually your unique gifts! Things that make you special.

Once you are willing to embrace your special qualities and leave behind your fake self, you are on your way to embracing your glorious future.

"Successful artists bring their authentic selves to their art every day!"

CHAPTER 18

YOU ARE THE PRODUCT!

"When you pursue acting, you're starting a business. In a business, you must fall in love with your product. You are the 'product'!"

When you walk through any famous shopping district, whether it's Rodeo Drive in Beverly Hills, Knightsbridge in London, or Via Condotti in Rome, there are many breathtaking stores that all have one thing in common—they all want you to walk in and buy something. Whether you enter the store or not is not just based on your needs. The store's particular appearance has the power to draw you in as well.

Potential *customers*, like casting directors, agents, producers, and directors, do not have time to go into every "store." In one of my Masterclasses, a top Hollywood publicist said, "It's not who you know that matters, it's who would want to know you." If you give off a feeling of being unapproachable, sad, and shy, you're not going to attract any customers. It doesn't matter what amazing quality of talent you're selling.

If they are not enticed to go into your store, they will never have the opportunity to buy anything from you. Stores sell products, and we sell our *talent, creativity, authenticity,* and, most importantly, our *humanity*!

Since there's such strong competition out there, your store, which is *you*, has to be energetically attractive and joyful.

Let's imagine that for a store to operate successfully, it needs ten departments. I want you to imagine that there are ten departments inside you. Think of them like employees working on your behalf. As the owner of your company, it's your job to inspire each department to perform at its very best.

If your employees show up to work and see that the owner, which is you, lacks passion, inspiration, energy, and vision, they will get very disheartened and become less productive. They won't work so hard because they know that there is no future in the company of "YOU," and this will trickle down all the way to your lower-ranking employees and departments. They will wish they were working for another company. To have a successful business, you must constantly be motivating your inner employees. You have to inspire them!

> *"The different departments must become a united team. Only by playing together with a common purpose, focus, and objective will you succeed."*

If they aren't working well together, it's because you haven't shown all the departments how to operate with one another efficiently, and you may be lacking the necessary leadership qualities. You will need to acquire those skills quickly to be able to survive bankruptcy!

Here are the ten departments that make up your store:

THE DEPARTMENT OF OPTIMISM

One of the secrets of all the top Fortune 500 companies is that each of them approaches business optimistically. They all see a positive future when others do not. They know that after a big rainstorm comes a rainbow. Now, if you can't remain optimistic, you're eventually going to fail. For others to be optimistic about *your* prospects, you first need to be optimistic about yourself and your future.

THE DEPARTMENT OF PASSION AND EMOTION

Your dream must be something you want to do more than anything else in the world. When you think about it, it should make you emotionally joyful. You feel that this profession is your life's mission, what you were born for. If your dream or goal doesn't set your soul on fire, then it's just an idea and it will never become a reality. Passion and emotion will push you through any kind of negativity or obstacles that will come your way. *Emotional people are unstoppable!*

THE DEPARTMENT OF FINANCE

You need to have a very good relationship with money. Instead of worrying about not having enough money, you need to believe that money will come—even when you're not exactly sure where it's coming from. Most people have a terrible relationship with money. You need money for the different aspects of your business. You need it for continuous training in acting, speech, dance, singing, improv, voice/dialect, and private coaching. They all require finances. Plus, you need to join a fitness club and get dynamic professional pictures that capture your uniqueness. Event clothes, transportation, and living expenses—you must see all of this as a worthy investment in you, and not as an expense. Many actors have created different streams of income to be able to support their career. *You will need to invest in yourself to increase the value of your company.*

THE DEPARTMENT OF PROBLEM SOLVING

There will always be problems in any business; that's a given. If you can't solve your problems creatively or by asking experts for help, your company will cease to operate. Remember, obstacles are the cost of excellence of any dream you pursue. The bigger the dream, the tougher the obstacle—*but* . . . the greater the reward. You need a strong department that focuses on solving issues quickly and effectively.

THE DEPARTMENT OF LOVING YOURSELF

The more you love yourself, the more you're willing to do for yourself. And when you really love yourself, that's when you will start valuing your gifts. Treat yourself with love and kindness, and watch your future change for the better instantly. Keep increasing your love toward your talent and gifts.

THE DEPARTMENT OF RISKS

The more risks you take, the more successful you will become. Taking risks will give you an exciting and adventurous life. That is a bit scary, but winners know that to win you have to be ready to lose. If you never want to lose, you will always lose. The greater the risk, the greater the reward!

THE DEPARTMENT OF ENJOYMENT

This is a very important department, which is most often neglected. If you don't find the joy in doing your job, then you're going to burn out. Bill Gates has a great long-term employee retention rate because he treats his employees very well. He knows that happy people make happier and more competent employees.

If you're constantly working without taking care of yourself, you're not going to be very productive. Stress kills! Watch the movie *Heal* to learn more about this. People who can't find joy in their profession will never reach the highest level of success in their career. Happiness is not a destination; happiness is an ongoing energy force that motivates your work and keeps you moving forward!

THE DEPARTMENT OF INSTINCTS

The Department of Instincts works this way—you feel compelled to do something, and you act on that feeling. Now, the mind will always see the negative side of everything you want to accomplish, and, if you let it, the mind will then control your every decision and, consequently, limit your future possibilities. It is your instincts and your heart that must tell the mind how to live—not the other way around. Steve Jobs was once fired from his own company because of his unique concepts, but he didn't shy away from what he set out to achieve, and we all know how that story turned out. He got his job back and was an even bigger success than before! Listen to your instincts. They're always right.

> *"Don't let the noise of other people's opinions drown out your own inner voice."* —Steve Jobs

THE DEPARTMENT OF RELATIONSHIPS

How well do you communicate with other people? How are your communication skills? Because we rely on electronic devices, verbal communication skills are being severely underdeveloped.

It's a serious problem.

Life, like acting, is all about communication, and if you are not constantly improving those skills, then you won't advance as an actor or as a human being. You must be able to convey all your needs, wants, and challenges effectively. This is not an easy thing to do. It's important to develop strong business relationships, and how you communicate within them will determine the success of your future career.

THE DEPARTMENT OF TRAINING

Every major company has training programs to teach their employees the latest techniques. I go around the world to teach CEOs, executives, and employees how to better deal with the ever-changing needs of "the customer." To maintain an edge in business, you have to constantly be learning and evolving. If you're not training or improving, you're becoming obsolete.

> **"If you don't get better as an actor, you're falling behind. Acting demands are constantly evolving."**

We have been honored to have the legendary Al Pacino speak to our Masterclasses. In one of the discussions, he mentioned that he's been seeing his acting coach once a week, every week, for the past thirty-five years! "I'm always open to learning," he said to the actors. That is why he is the ultimate artist.

If Al Pacino is still learning and working on his craft every week, then what's stopping you? We are very fortunate to have had him share his insight and wisdom with us after screening his acclaimed films *Chinese Coffee*, *Salomé*, and *Wilde Salomé*. I recommend that you watch them. It was an unforgettable experience!

In Europe, where I have worked for many years, some actors do not realize that they need to *continue* their training. They get a diploma from an acting school, and when they get a job or join a theatre company they somehow think, *Well, that's it! That's all I needed to learn.* If you don't keep improving as an actor, you will eventually become irrelevant in this business. The demands of the craft of acting are always changing. Getting powerful training is one of the Hollywood rules that all committed actors adhere to as a way to stay ahead of the competition.

FIND YOUR MISSION STATEMENT

To find your mission statement, start by asking yourself these questions: What is my heart/instinct telling me that I should be pursuing? What gives me the utmost joy and fulfills my purpose? What profession would I be happy doing, even if I wasn't getting paid? Listen for the answers and keep asking more questions until you find your mission.

For any business to be successful, it must also benefit others in some way. Your mission statement must be so meaningful and emotional that you don't need any motivation to pursue it. You *love* working on all the different parts of your craft, and it doesn't feel like a job.

> *"We make a living by what we get. We make a life by what we give." —Winston Churchill*

This is a profession that you must be willing to devote your life to, and there must be nothing more artistically satisfying for you. (Read chapter thirty-four, "Look Out, World!," in order to understand how your art must benefit the world.)

> *"The two most important days of your life are the day you are born and the day you find out why!" —Mark Twain*

CHAPTER 19

LOVE & HAPPINESS ARE SERIOUS BUSINESS

Happiness and love should be the driving force to achieve the things you truly desire. There is a huge myth out there that happiness only occurs when you finally achieve your goals or dreams. In fact, it's the other way around.

Did you know that happiness is something you have within you—right now? We were all born as bundles of joy, but as we get older, we become influenced by outside forces. Forces like society, family, friends, and the world. They told us that we would only be happy if we attain certain material things in our lives, such as money, fame, or security. Although these things can give you a temporary high, they quickly fade away.

The only thing that keeps you from experiencing happiness right now is your thoughts and feelings toward it. The reason this feeling is so important is that, as I have observed, genuinely happy people discover more of their talents and gifts and bring more light to every situation.

Love is also clouded by another one of those myths, which states that you will feel love when you meet the right person or find the right job. Love isn't something that you'll just find outside of yourself; it actually lives within you—right now too!

In order to bring more love and happiness into your life, you first have to embrace all that you are. Feeling happy and loving yourself is the starting point, but you must release your anger and sadness to make more room for love and joy! Once you express those dark feelings, it frees you from the pain and difficulties of the past.

In the everyday decisions you make, ask yourself, "Am I making this choice out of love or out of fear?" Know that you were created from love and that you ARE LOVE. Love feeds and nurtures our soul, which is why we desire it. Have the courage to love yourself every day, and when you do, you'll find you care more about your life and others.

When you live with love and happiness, you will know what you were born to do, and your purpose and meaning will become clear. You will feel successful. Therefore, you will succeed, because you know that this is your destiny. Love unlocks your true potential. It brings attention to the miracles around you, and you feel guided to make the world a better place. What you share and give to the world stays forever!

Know that loving yourself is a *daily habit*! To start loving yourself, you must:

1. Stop criticizing yourself.

2. Learn to say "No" when you have to and let go of negative relationships.

3. Write a love letter to yourself.

4. Try something new that brings excitement into your life.

5. Eat great food and treat your body like a temple.

Also, make a list of the things that you need to do to increase and maintain your happiness and love. Commit to taking actions daily that produce these feelings. Only when you take active steps to increase love, self-worth, and joy will you be on the path to your success.

> *"Love yourself first because that's who you'll be spending the rest of your life with."*

CHAPTER 20

SURPRISE, SURPRISE, BLOCKS & FEARS ARE GREAT

When it comes to blocks and fears, people think, *Wow, these are terrible*, but the truth is your blocks and fears are gifts from your soul to help you discover your strengths and make you stronger. They have been placed in your path for you to work on your own personal growth. These are things that you will need to overcome to get to your next level. Once you overcome your blocks and fears, you discover your inner power. Only powerful people can achieve incredible things in life.

When my students tell me, "I want to have more confidence," I always reply with, "Well, you have to do things that you're afraid to do. That's the only way you'll discover newfound confidence."

Now, turn all your fears into questions. For example: "I feel that I'm not good enough to succeed in this career." Change that fearful thought into a question. "Am I good enough to succeed in this career?" I don't know. *You* will need to find out. "I feel that people won't like me." Turn that fearful thought into a question. "Will people like me?" *You* will need to find out. And, "I don't have the courage to ask for help." Turn that into a question and find out. "Do I have the courage to ask for help?" I don't know. Try it. When you turn your fears into a question, you'll discover a clear action you must take to help you overcome that fear. That puts you in control of overcoming F.E.A.R.: False Evidence Appearing Real. Now, if you don't answer these questions, all you are left with are your fears. Only *you* have the power to find the answers to all of your questions. Fears are feelings, not facts.

As a child, you are actually born with only two fears: the fear of loud noises and the fear of falling. All other fears you now have were given, accepted, and embraced by you. Fears live in your head as a feeling that something in the future will not turn out well. The more you live in your head, the more fears you will have.

> *"Everything you've ever wanted is on the other side of fear." —George Addair*

Blocks are limitations placed on your path—by YOU! A block such as "I'm not good enough" stops a lot of people. Now, of course, that's ridiculous because you're reading this book, and you obviously know that, deep down inside, you *are* good enough. The reason you place a block like that in your path is because you are protecting yourself from the pain of failing, so you don't even try. But when you protect yourself from the pain of failure, you also prevent success, joy, and happiness from entering your life. Imagine what you could achieve with the right mindset, training, and attitude.

Les Brown says, "You have greatness inside," and he's right! You need the courage to find your greatness and to release the mental blocks that are in your way. Blocks and fears are *not* bad. Yes, they are negative, but only if you don't do anything about them. However, they're liberating once you face and deal with them. Stay vigilant by continually overcoming your blocks and fears as they come your way. That's when you grow and become the powerful artist and person you were always meant to be.

There are only two types of people in the world: people who are afraid and act, and people who are just afraid. Now, which one will you choose to be?

> ### *"If you give your life a chance, it will prove all your fears wrong."*

Steve Jobs said it best:

> *"Here's to the crazy ones, the misfits, the rebels, the troublemakers, the round pegs in the square holes, the ones who see things differently. They are not fond of rules, and they have no respect for the status quo. You can quote them, disagree with them, glorify or vilify them. About the only thing you can't do is ignore them because they change things."*

CHAPTER 21

THE BENEFITS OF NEGATIVITY

What is the definition of the word *benefit?* Well, something that is beneficial is advantageous to *you* in some way. Other people may not see the benefits of your behavior, thinking, or actions, but you do—consciously or subconsciously. People always believe that their actions, thoughts, or reactions will be beneficial to them in some way. No one ever does or chooses anything that they think will not be good for them. Based on their mindset, they always find some kind of benefit.

Students always tell me that they wish they trusted themselves more or weren't so afraid, when, in actuality, they hang onto their negative thinking and behavior because they find it beneficial.

What could possibly be good about not believing in YOURSELF?

Well, if you don't believe in yourself, then you won't pursue your dreams and you won't get hurt, disappointed, or feel any kind of sorrow. Unfortunately, you're tragically mistaken. All "negative" habits you have right now are choices *you* have made for yourself. Choices that you think will keep you protected from pain, shame, or criticism. Know that no one is born with any negative thoughts. They are ideas that you have adopted or were given. Every unhelpful or helpful habit you now have is something that you have chosen to keep and believe in because it serves you in some way. For example, if you take drugs or drink excessively, you may not perceive them as destructive behaviors. You may use drugs or alcohol to escape your life momentarily, to forget your current situation, or because they make you feel good. They may give you the freedom to do some things you would not be able to do if you were sober. Drugs and alcohol are therefore beneficial to those who keep taking them.

You can justify any action by telling yourself that it's the right thing for *you* to do. So, what's so good about living in pain or sadness? Well, for some people, sadness and pain bring attention from others—it's a way for you to connect or disconnect. In life, we all strive for attention. There's nothing wrong with this innate need. We are all trying to get attention in some way, be it through our positive or negative behavior. However, in some foreign countries that I have worked in, I have met actors who told me that their society's way of connecting to others is through their pain and sadness.

> ### "When you argue for your limitations, you get to keep them!"

THE "I WISH" EXERCISE

First, write down five personality traits that you wish would disappear today. These are traits you are convinced that, once gone, would make your life instantly improve and get better. Not material things, or how other people behave—your personal negative habits. For example:

I wish I were more open.

I wish I were more courageous.

I wish I believed in myself.

I wish I felt I was talented.

I wish I weren't so afraid to talk to new people.

Now, rewrite those statements in the affirmative.

I like not being open.

I like not being courageous.

I like not believing in myself.

I like feeling that I am not talented.

I like not talking to new people.

You see, you are wishing that these negative behaviors would just leave, but that's not *really* true, because the truth is you actually like them in some subconscious way. They serve some kind of purpose for you.

So, let's focus on one of your habits to show you what I mean:

"I wish I were more open."

Now, list all the benefits of not being open, this so-called negative behavior.

Some students answer quickly, "Bernard, there aren't any benefits," and I say, "Search, and you will definitely find them because nobody in the world does anything without some kind of benefit." This is due to your upbringing, education, society, belief system, and the amount of love and encouragement you've received growing up.

Now, from your point of view, make a list of all the benefits of your negative behavior.

Benefits of *not* being open!

It protects me from being rejected and being in pain.

I can feel comfortable by not taking any risks.

I don't have to become vulnerable.

My lack of openness gives me attention. People ask me, "What's wrong?" Or I'm ignored, and then no one can judge me.

I don't have to learn or grow because change is scary. I can relax and maintain what I have.

Now, find the benefits of your new, positive behavior. Until you see increased benefits in this positive behavior, you'll refuse to move forward with this new way of thinking. A successful life always starts with powerful thoughts, actions, and courage—including a willingness to accept being vulnerable and living in uncertainty.

Now, make a list of the benefits of being open.

Benefits of being open!
I could meet people who might improve my life and career.

I could be open for loving relationships.

I could let joy, happiness, and fulfillment find me, which feeds my soul.

I could learn, grow, and change for the better. Constant improvements keep me desirable to others.

I could be open to accepting miracles that create new opportunities.

I could feel my feelings and become emotional. Emotional people are powerful and unstoppable.

Only when you believe that the list of benefits from the "positive" behaviors outweighs the list of "negative" behaviors will you change. However, you have to discover the value in these benefits yourself. No one can force you to change.

You will know if you made the wrong choices if your life is not flowing and if you are not living your most creative and successful life.

Once you have found the benefits of your new behavior, you have to practice and encourage this way of thinking.

Let me show you how to get rid of those old, negative habits.

1. You have to speak to your *negative* habits kindly and sweetly, and say, "Thank you for keeping me safe. I thought our relationship was working, but now I see there is a new way that I must try. I'm sorry, but I will have to let you go." Don't get upset or angry when you speak to your old habits because you have welcomed them into your life, and they have lived inside your head rent-free for years! Know that those negative thoughts and behaviors will not just simply vanish, never to be seen again. They will wait patiently in the shadows for the right moment when you call them back into your life. When you're stressed, feeling sad, or when chaos and fear rule the day, that's when they'll come knocking!

2. New habits, like the old habits, are created by you because you see the benefits. Connect to the benefits of the new ways of thinking. These new behaviors will always lead you to the road that you've been looking for. Your new habits need your support and commitment.

3. "Fake it until you make it" means just that. At the beginning of adopting these new habits, it's going to feel strange and uncomfortable. However, over time, they will become second nature to you. When this happens, you'll realize that dreams can come true if you see the benefits!

It takes consistent practice, dedication, and a newfound love for yourself to maintain the benefits of the positive behaviors, and then your life changes for the better instantly. Realize that when you were protecting yourself from pain, you were also protecting yourself from all the joys, magic, and opportunities that life has to offer you as well.

"You suffer forever for all the actions in life that you did not take!"

Why does anyone continue with their negative habits? Well, it's because they don't love themselves enough to stop these habits; sadly, some people are actually addicted to their pain, suffering, or negativity.

These habits are protection mechanisms that you have created, keeping you from being vulnerable in a world that is frightening. By creating negative habits, you think you are guarding yourself against suffering, but, in fact, they hurt you more than you may think and you end up with more pain, which is the thing you have been so desperately trying to avoid.

The opposite of negativity is vulnerability. This is your key to removing your negative habits. To be vulnerable is to be open and take risks. If you want all the possibilities and excitement that life has to offer, you must expose your heart and accept being the true you.

There is no other way around it. Yes, you run the risk of feeling pain and rejection, but you could also experience great joy, love, and success. Only when you are in the state of *vulnerability* can you achieve your dreams or goals.

"Out of your vulnerabilities will come your strength." —*Sigmund Freud*

It's interesting that Freud said you must first be vulnerable, and then you'll be able to discover your power and strength. When you first thought about your dreams and wondered if they could actually come true, your mind began giving you all the reasons why they could never happen. So, some dreams and goals were quashed even before they began. This happens when you live in your head.

THE 20/80 RULE

Let's talk about the 20-to-80 percent rule. Pain is part of life, and by trying to avoid pain, you are also closing yourself off to all the incredible and unforgettable things that life has to offer. Let's say you see someone at a party that you'd like to speak to, but you're afraid to approach this person because he or she might reject you. So you stay back and say nothing. You think that by not approaching you won't be hurt from the situation, but truthfully, you've avoided an opportunity, which will hurt you forever.

In life, we all have two choices to make: either a possibility of 20 percent of temporary pain, or 80 percent of pain lasting FOREVER. Which one do you think is better? If the person you approached had said no, that could have hurt you 20 percent, but since you didn't ask them, you will suffer 80 percent pain. FOREVER! That's crazy!

Not knowing what they would have said and what this relationship could have been will haunt you forever. It's the same with any business action or life question that you didn't have the courage to pursue.

Inaction, at the moment that you needed to act, will emotionally kill you for a lifetime!

"When you numb your pain, you also numb your joy." —Brené Brown

"The person who's willing to be truly vulnerable WINS, in every area of their life!

CHAPTER 22

FROZEN IN A PLACE WHERE NOTHING GROWS

"Nothing happens until something moves." —Albert Einstein

There comes a time in your life where you feel restless, unsatisfied, and you suspect that you are living in your comfort zone. It is a lifeless and empty place that you have stayed in for far too long. Your heart says, "There's more to life than this!" but your mind says, "Play it safe. Don't rock the boat. Stay where you are, and guard what you have!"

"Comfort zones are where all your dreams, talents, and ideas go to die."

When you're in this "dead zone," you find yourself functioning without energy, meaning, or purpose. It's an awful place to be. Unfortunately, so many people accept living in this lifeless place and consider it their "normal" state.

We live in a world where fear is the dominant experience. So, to counterbalance this, you seek a *false* sense of security.

You fear the unknown, and you're too frightened to open yourself up to the possibilities of something great occurring in your life because you believe that whatever's in your future will never be as good as what you have right now. Trust me, nothing is further from the truth!

You were created with limitless possibilities. That's not a bumper sticker; it's a fact! The way to achieve your potential is to overcome your own fears so you can accomplish your intended goals. It's only a matter of time before you realize that you must leave your comfort zones in order to flourish, or you will die there. If you are not taking action to move your life forward, you will remain stuck forever and never live the life you were born to achieve!

> *"In order to discover new lands, one must be willing to lose sight of the shore." —André Gide*

So, why are so many of you stuck?

Well, it's because you are emotionally disconnected from knowing or expressing your feelings. Emotions are our bodies' power source. And how did you become so disconnected? It comes from having traumatic events from your past, perhaps experiences from childhood. With help and advice, you must retrace the steps of the past to free yourselves. As life continues to unfold, there will always be something for you to work through to move forward toward greater success.

But before you can start moving forward, you must first look back. You were born perfect and living in a world full of excitement and possibilities, but once you were highly criticized and learned societal and family constraints, you lost your true self and started to disconnect from your feelings.

If you were made to feel ashamed or humiliated for expressing your feelings, ideas, and emotions as a child, you then disconnected from your voice and your inner power. Other reasons for disconnecting include having been neglected or experiencing physical, emotional, or other abuses. All of these can cause you to lose your strength and identity.

Les Brown, the great motivational speaker, whom I had the honor to work with many times, said, "To discover your real voice, you must have the courage to tell the truth about the difficult things that have happened to you." And he's absolutely right! Speaking the truth strengthens your voice.

Finding your emotions is the essential element that you'll need on your journey. Emotions act as an energy conductor. Without emotions, nothing moves. When you let others define you, confusion, low self-worth, and weakness become your normal state.

You need to understand that your subconscious contains a powerful mechanism that allows you to distance yourself from your own feelings and emotions. When painful emotions get too overwhelming for you, this *safety mechanism* allows you to disconnect, and you will not want to reconnect. This problem will stop your life and career. You must seek professional help to guide you past this safety block so that you can live life and dream again. It will be hard work, but it is work that must be done.

When you stay disconnected from your emotions, you're also disconnecting from your energy, talent, purpose, and authentic self. When you feel lost, confused, and unable to commit to any direction, it is because you are disconnected from your instincts and your heart. People who are disconnected from their pain and sorrow may think that their pain has disappeared, but they're mistaken. All unresolved trauma, sadness, and pain needs to be addressed and expressed. Otherwise, it will only increase and be harder to overcome. Left unattended, this will lead to a wide range of complications—ranging from reccurring illnesses to anxiety, panic attacks, insomnia, fear of physical contact, lack of self-worth, depression, and possibly a mental breakdown. There are some wonderful therapists out there that can help you with this. Once you clear up these issues, you can get back on track to pursue your dreams, goals, and life.

One of the more serious symptoms of emotional disconnection is that you bottled up your feelings, leaving your body drained and fatigued. When the suppression of your true feelings reaches a boiling point, you explode with anger, which is not productive or beneficial for anyone involved.

I have worked and coached around the globe, and it is clear to me that certain cultures and societies have a very negative opinion of expressing one's emotions. Emotions are even considered a sign of weakness. As a result, people work on keeping their emotions bottled up and under control. They believe that anger or sadness are never good emotions to express. Some try to stop feeling anything at all, which is like holding your breath. Eventually, you have to let it out.

You can't stop feeling, but you can stop expressing how you feel. Which will end up killing you emotionally and even cause physical ailments and diseases.

Mistakenly, the emotional focus in many countries is to rationalize feelings by only using the mind to make decisions. Not using your heart or instincts to make decisions will lead to a life of monotony and missing out on your life's real purpose and possibilities.

> ### *"Whatever emotions you cannot express control your life."*

It takes an understanding and exploration of your entire emotional spectrum to be fully alive. Your emotions have direct connection to your body, whether you are listening to them or not.

> ### *"Once you plug into your emotional body, you are connected to your life force."*

CHAPTER 23

QUICK, OPEN THE DOOR!

"There is nothing more expensive in life than a missed opportunity."

Opportunities don't knock; they whisper. You will need a quiet mind and a sensitive soul to connect to them. Only by eliminating anger, negativity, and sadness from your life will you know that opportunities are all around you. If you absorb this book's information passionately and sincerely, and truly take it to heart, it will turn into a transformational opportunity.

"Opportunities are the things that change lives for the better!"

Instincts will lead you to your opportunities. You can't see or touch instincts. They often appear illogical and contradictory. However, if you constantly live in your doubts and fears, you will never hear, feel, or see the opportunities that are around you. Only by living in the NOW will you connect with your instincts.

Most people are stopped on their path because their minds tell them that their dreams are ridiculous and unattainable. Of course, they are wrong!

"If you ever feel that your dream is too BIG—then it's because your mind is too SMALL."

Opportunities come in all shapes and sizes. They will come from places you least expect. Reading this chapter could be a big opportunity if you want it to. Great dreams come with an equal amount of negativity and difficulty trying to stop you. They are there to challenge you and help you discover how *serious* you are about your dream. When you avoid your opportunities, you deny yourself the life that is in store for you.

Successful artists face the same problems as everyone else, but they are determined to triumph despite anything or anyone trying to stop them. I have found that actors who take responsibility for their lives and careers succeed.

"What are you doing today that your future self will thank you for?"

WHY DO PEOPLE MISS THEIR OPPORTUNITIES?

Write down five missed opportunities that you have had in your life.

Missed opportunities are moments in time when you realize you should have said something to someone, and behaved or reacted in a certain way, but you didn't seize "that moment" because your doubts or fears got in the way. You feel bad, even now, thinking about them.

Know that every opportunity that comes your way is forcing you to change, learn, and grow. When you refuse to do this, you miss out on reaching your full potential and, in turn, your destiny!

Below are five lessons you must learn to reap the benefits of your opportunities to achieve your goals and dreams.

LESSON 1

When opportunities present themselves, they are forcing you to become more courageous. To succeed in these moments, you must be more courageous than you've ever been before. *Courage is action over fear*. It's been said that twenty seconds of newfound courage can dramatically change your career and life forever. I'm sure you can generate twenty more courageous seconds!

LESSON 2

Opportunities also force you to be in a state of uncertainty. Give up the idea of control. Accept uncertainty, or you will miss your opportunities.

LESSON 3

Opportunities are forcing you to disconnect from your mind and connect directly to your instincts. Your instincts are trying to guide you to your success. Your mind lives in fear. Instincts come from your loving heart. They are calling you, but you must be willing to listen and take that leap of faith.

LESSON 4

Opportunities force you to believe more in yourself. You must increase your self-worth in order to increase the quality of your life. If you want more out of life, you have to believe that you are worth more!

LESSON 5

Opportunities force you to take action. Stop waiting, making excuses, or blaming others. Take an action today that you know you should have done yesterday; call, email, or connect with someone who will present you with your next opportunity.

> *"Every man takes the limits of his own field of vision for*
> *the limits of the world." —Arthur Schopenhauer*

Know that every great dream or goal comes into fruition through opportunities.

"When you become unrealistic, you succeed."

CHAPTER 24

IT'S TIME TO PLANT SEEDS

Farmers know that if you don't plant in the spring, there won't be a harvest in the fall. As artists, we must do exactly the same thing. If you are not planting seeds of opportunity everywhere you go, you will have nothing to feed your career, goals, or dreams. Planting seeds is the secret to any successful career. That's what I try to do all the time.

Planting starts by meeting new people, creating projects, helping others, taking Masterclasses, going to seminars, and saying "YES" to all opportunities, readings, or meetings that come your way.

If you want to harvest a great life for your future, you must plant and cultivate now to get there. For seeds to grow to maturity, you must supply them with good earth, water, sunshine, and plenty of loving attention. If you don't nourish your ideas, they will die. Also, if you only plant one or two seeds, you'll reduce your opportunities, leading to dismay, frustration, and anxiety.

So, if you're feeling frustrated, nervous, and anxious, it's because you haven't planted enough seeds. Consequently, if you plant an abundant field of opportunities everywhere you go, then you're always living in a state of positive anticipation, gladly waiting for something exciting to happen.

Of course, some seeds of opportunity may not come to fruition, but that doesn't matter. As long as you just keep planting something every day, eventually something will blossom and grow. It's a numbers game!

You also shouldn't label any outcome as strictly good or bad because you never know where that particular journey will take you. Some leads take you in a different direction that can turn out to be so much better for you than you anticipated. This has happened to me personally so many times. Know that whatever has been placed in your way, it's to test you to see your level of commitment about what you desire. It may send you on an alternative path to get there, but trust the process and don't fight against the current.

Having patience is also something you will need after planting. Patience is something I had to learn to cultivate. Marvelous things do take time! They don't grow overnight. Did you know? Chinese bamboo can take five years before breaking soil, and then suddenly, in its fifth year, it grows ninety feet in about a month!

Know that whatever you give your energy, love, and attention to will grow. If you keep planting for the future, your life will be forever thriving.

> *"Don't judge each day by the harvest you reap but by the seeds that you plant."* —*Robert Louis Stevenson*

TURN A "NO" INTO A "NOW"!

If you're pursuing a dream or goal, and a word like "NO" can stop you, then the truth is, it's not for you. Those who are emotionally connected to *why* their dreams are so important cannot be stopped!

> *"If anything can stop you from being an actor then it's not for you."* —Neil Simon

One of the things you will hear throughout your entire life is the word "NO." When average people hear this, they accept it, stop pursuing their dreams, and believe dreams are impossible. If you can't overcome this simple two-letter word, nothing will manifest in your life.

I have taught all my students that when they hear the word "NO," they need to think that the other person just said "NOW!" Your job is to push your agenda even further, finding creative ways to connect with that person, and change their mind.

Saying no has become an automatic response for people across the world. In a way, everything you've ever wanted starts with no, and it's your job to turn every no into a YES!

Whatever you have now, you have created. If something's not there, it's because YOU haven't created it yet. I have many superstar guests that share their journey and insights in my Masterclasses and seminars around the world, and many have shared that the noes they received while pursuing their career pushed them harder to succeed. This practice really works!

I present my students with a fun challenge. I tell them to go to the best restaurant in town, where getting a table can take months, and dine there—tonight! Their job is to change a "No, I'm sorry, we are fully booked" into an "Of course, right this way!"

So, how do they achieve this?

There are only three ways. You have to use your charm, humility, and humor. This idea I got from acting coach Uta Hagen, who said, "If a person can't do a small thing, they'll never be able to accomplish a big thing." If you can't accomplish something small, like getting a table at a busy restaurant, do you actually think you'll be able to overcome all the challenges, rejection, and difficulties in pursuing a successful acting career?

Find the challenge in overcoming each obstacle, and find new tactics to make this happen. Look, you might disturb some people along the way, but as the old saying goes, "You can't make an omelet without breaking a few eggs." I guarantee you that you will feel a lifetime of regret for all the things you did not do!

Les Brown said something remarkable: "If you make easy choices in life, you'll have a hard life, but if you make hard choices in life, you'll have an easy life." So, ask yourself, "What quality of life am I experiencing right now?"

Hard choices need to be made to live the life you always wanted, like walking away from a bad relationship, leaving your comfort zones, moving from your hometown, leaving the job that's killing you, or starting your artistic journey. All of these things can be painful. Know that a lot of hard work takes place before success happens. Accepting the pain that comes for the sake of growth, daring to express your feelings by telling the truth, and, more importantly, living your authentic self are just some of the hard choices that you will have to face to change your life for the better! Trust me, it's worth it.

Average people see high walls and know they'll never make it over. Successful people see high walls and know they will overcome them in one way or another to live the life they were born for.

> *"If you are not ready to fight for what you want, you automatically get what you don't want!"*

CHAPTER 26

GOING THE WRONG WAY ON THE RIGHT ROAD?

Some people are fortunate enough to find the path that will help them succeed in life, but unfortunately, some approach the road to their success by shifting into reverse! Therefore, they won't get any of the benefits that the path has to offer.

Here are some ways you can tell if you are going the wrong way on the right road.

1. You enter a class, a project, or a business relationship with your negative issues. You bring your trauma, sadness, or pessimism to the journey. You're living in your past and you brought nothing to the present that anyone can use. So, understandably, people will soon let you go.

2. You're too scared to emotionally commit to your dream, idea, or goal. The mind despises pressure and pain, and therefore avoids tough problems and situations as much as it can. Remember, it takes pressure to make a diamond!

3. You're not expecting *miracles*. Miracles are the crucial ingredients that you need for your dreams and goals to materialize. Be open to receive them.

4. You keep believing that your dream is just too crazy. Know that crazy dreams *won't happen* unless you can turn those dreams into reality. Otherwise, your lack of believing is making them unattainable. You need to know that there is always someone out there who is living the dream you want. Always! Your dreams might be crazy for others, but you must start to feel and believe that they are normal. With the right actions, transformation, and coaching, they are within your grasp.

5. You are not seeking guidance. All great success stories include the day their mentor or acting coach helped change their career forever. Go find yours!

    "A mentor is someone who can take you to a place within yourself—that you could never go by yourself." —Les Brown

6. You care too much about what others think. It's not their dream. It's YOURS! Don't talk about what you are *going* to do. Just do it!

7. You don't believe you can overcome the obstacles in your path. To succeed, you must feel that no matter what obstacles you encounter along the way, you'll be able to handle them because you are the *exception* to every rule. Your talent and gifts are unique, but *only* if you keep developing them.

8. You're too afraid. If all your actions are motivated by fear, nothing good can ever come from them.

Listen to your intuition. Let it tell you when you're going in the wrong direction. When life starts to flow and fall into place, and you're filled with joy, you're heading in the right direction.

> *"If you don't know where you're going, any road will take you there."* —George Harrison

CHAPTER 27

IT'S NOT ME—IT'S YOU!

When you're in pain due to a breakup or a misfortune, or when things are not going your way, you can easily point your finger at everyone else and say, "Hey, it's not my fault. It's the fault of my family, friends, lover, teachers, neighbors, society, or the people who are controlling the industry."

What you may not realize is that when you point your finger at everyone else (like a gun), three fingers are pointing back at YOU. Try it and see.

I'm sorry to tell you, but it's always YOU. Not me—not them. Just YOU!

Why do we blame others? Well, we blame them because it is an excellent defense mechanism. Instead of seeing your own inadequacies and facing the flaws that you need to work on, you go around blaming others. I know that this can be frustrating to accept, but when you are one of those people who always think, *I'm not responsible for this situation in any way*, you lose your power. If you blame anyone or anything for your current situation, it makes you weak.

If something is wrong, only you can change it. The moment you come to terms with this fact will be the moment you find your inner power. Only powerful people can change their own lives. If it's always *everyone else's fault*, then your problems will last forever.

I know that there are some moments in life where you are rendered powerless with the terrible circumstances you are in, where it was not your fault in any way; but how you respond to the pain, crisis, drama, lack of success, or failure IS your responsibility.

> *"Know that your destiny is always bigger than*
> *your day." —Dr. Sean McMillan*

Take your power back, and watch your life change for the better. Of course, this is not always easy to do, but life never throws you something you can't figure out with time, love, wisdom, and creativity.

You are never your current circumstances. As soon as you say to yourself, "It is me," then you start taking the journey inward. Ask yourself: "Am I working hard enough?" Or, "Am I working smart enough?" And, "Am I learning, training, being vulnerable, positive, and taking risks?"

A lot of intense work will need to be done. Therefore, seek professional guidance. Our studio teaches actors how to reach their goals and live their dreams—AWAKE!

"You might be studying, meditating, or yoga retreating, but if you don't change your thinking, behavior, and actions—you'll fail."

CHAPTER 28

STRANGERS ARE FRIENDS YOU HAVEN'T MET

To become successful in this business, you must talk to a lot of people that you don't know because in Hollywood or any industry, your level of success runs on your ability to interact and connect with others. You will need lots of help from others to achieve anything great. I'm grateful and thankful to the hundreds of people who have helped and been so kind to me along my journey.

Now, how you first approach someone will determine whether you fail or succeed with them. Everyone judges you by the first impression you make, and you never get a second chance to make a first impression! It is extremely important that you understand this. When you walk up to someone, ask yourself this question: "Is this person I'm going up to a friend or a stranger?"

If you decide "stranger," you will act in a strange way when you speak to them. If you decide "friend," you will act more friendly toward them. Which do you think is going to be more effective?

How do you enter a room full of good friends you're excited to see? You're open, giving, happy, and enthusiastic. Now, practice these characteristics when you meet someone new. Of course, some of you may say, "I don't know this person that I'm about to talk to," but is this really true? Are you sure you don't know them? What is it that you don't know about them?

> **"Everyone in the world has the same needs and desires. Everyone wants to be loved, accepted, and understood. THAT'S EVERYONE ON EARTH!"**

So, this person isn't unknown to you, not really. Successful people see themselves in everyone they meet. Unsuccessful people will always feel that they are too different and that nobody will understand them. By really looking and connecting with the people you're talking to, you will be able to understand 85 percent of who they are.

Find people interesting, and they will find you interesting as well. They will have the same reaction you give them. One of my teachers once taught me that you should learn at least two minutes on every topic in the world so that when you meet new people, you can talk about anything. It's time to get busy learning lots of new things.

> *"I'm curious about people. That's the essence of my acting. I'm interested in what it would be like to be you."* —Meryl Streep

How you view other people will determine the degree of success you will have. So, start speaking to people that you don't know—as friends.

In fact, talk to three new people every day. That's the only way you're going to keep improving the art of communication.

Your mother was right—you shouldn't talk to strangers. So, talk to new people as though you genuinely know them. I love talking to new people. I learn so much from them, and I hope one day I get a chance to talk to you!

CHAPTER 29

REMEMBER NOT TO FORGET!

You are the most powerful person in your world, but you need to access your inner power to discover your amazing talents and uniqueness.

Here is a list of ways to keep supporting, encouraging, and achieving your greatness:

1. You must be investing time, energy, and money in yourself. It shows the world that you believe in your future success.

2. Stay connected to your heart and instincts. Creativity doesn't come from you; it consists of messages that *find you* the more open and joyful you are. Being stressed, sad, or angry will stop this creative process.

3. Charge your "happiness battery" daily. Do things every morning that make you happy, like listening to music, dancing, or talking to friends who make you laugh.

Throughout the day, read or watch something that motivates and inspires you. When you live in this energetic, alive state, people will want to be around you. Positive energy is contagious!

4. It's crucial to have uplifting colleagues and artists around you and to be an inspiring friend to others.

5. Write a positive email to yourself. Remind yourself of the special qualities you have and how you will nurture and encourage them. Also, describe *why* you will be able to realize your goals and dreams.

6. Don't just focus on *what* you want, but more importantly, focus on the kind of person you need to become in order to *get* what you want.

7. Forge deep connections with passionate and dynamic people in your industry. That will determine your level of success.

8. You must find places for your talents, ideas, and authenticity to shine and be acknowledged.

9. Ask yourself, "What are the most loving things I can do for myself today?" Become more sensitive to your wants, needs, and feelings. Then you'll be able to make a stronger impact on the world and others.

10. Have the courage to continue being the REAL YOU! When you live your true, authentic self, you are open to the possibilities and opportunities that the universe is sending

you. Living in authenticity gives you the strength to do all of the above steps.

Many of you reading this book would like a life-changing moment. After such a moment, you will never be the same again, and your trajectory toward a successful life and career will change forever. If you apply the ten things listed above and other advice given throughout this book, you will have the life-changing moment you've been looking for. It's time to change your life for the better, not only because you deserve it, but because the world does.

MY LIFE-CHANGING MOMENT!

I was inspired to become an actor when I was seven years old after hearing this incredible true story from a Jewish man, who was living in Salonika, Greece. His story showed me the transformational power of acting. On this fateful day, during World War II, the National Socialist German Party—the Nazis—occupied Greece and began rounding up Jews to send to the concentration camps. He was running for his life when soldiers rounded a corner and spotted him in the middle of the street. The soldiers saw him, and he saw them. He felt a panic come over him and didn't know what to do or where to go. There was nowhere to hide!

As they came closer, to grab him for deportation, he immediately contorted every part of his body into a state of physical and mental disability. This man wasn't an actor, but in one extraordinary moment, he realized that he had to convincingly become someone else or he would surely lose his life. As one Nazi grabbed him, another soldier said, "Forget him. He's not even human." They miraculously left him behind and moved on to others. Acting literally saved his life, and his story, which I never forgot, inspired mine.

"Acting can save a life."

CHAPTER 30

EIGHT VITAL NEEDS

A major reason most people never achieve their dreams is that their subconscious energies are focused on their primal needs, which are not being taken care of. There are eight human needs that need to be satisfied. These needs will supersede any dream or goal you may have. Once fulfilled, you can focus all your energy on your passion and career.

FOOD & WATER

Your body is always in survival mode, constantly monitoring and thinking about food and water and where, when, and how you're going to get it. Now, if you didn't know where you were going to get your next meal, then this would become your primary goal. You would spend all of your time in search of sustenance, and you wouldn't be able to focus on anything else.

SHELTER & CLOTHING

What if you had no idea where you were going to sleep tonight? Could you honestly concentrate on reading this? I don't think so. One of the reasons that you feel calm enough to read right now is because you know you have a place to sleep and clothes to wear.

TO LOVE & BE LOVED

We all need love; it's not a choice. You love because you have to, not just because you want to. Your body and heart are constantly in search of love. Your soul keeps asking, "Where is my love?" You must be able to give and receive love to be fulfilled.

TO BE TOUCHED & TO BE HELD

This is a need that starts from the day that you are born. The first thing a doctor does when a baby is born is put them on their mother's chest because they need human contact. If you had a baby and you gave it food, attention, and clothing, but never touched or held your baby in the first year of its life, he or she would likely develop severe mental and psychological problems. In some cases, your baby could even die. What extinguishes love? The lack of human touch.

Studies have shown that the more children are lovingly held, the smarter and the more confident they become. Science suggests that we need at least five hugs a day. Are you getting yours?

ACKNOWLEDGING YOUR PAIN

The absence of accepting your deep hurts and not dealing with them will cause you more pain, as this messenger demands your immediate attention. If you feel angry, empty, sad, lonely, or worthless, you're not acknowledging your inner pain. You're trying to do what most people do by pretending that it doesn't exist. As much as you are trying to forget the pain, the pain never seems to forget you! That's because your body stores all the traumatic experiences you've had your entire life in your physical body and mind. Without acknowledging and releasing those hurtful feelings that are inside you, you won't be able to move on. The pain will keep getting worse until you deal with it.

BEING NEEDED

This is really what a family or community is all about. A family structure is having the feeling that you are wanted and needed, and you feel stronger together than you would feel being apart. If you don't feel like anyone needs or wants you, there's little reason to get up in the morning. There are very few things you can accomplish on your own, but with inspiring people, you can achieve anything. You want to belong to a group where people's eyes light up when they see you and they say things like, "We are so glad you're here!" and "We acknowledge and love who you are!" When you find this, you've found your creative family!

CREATING A LIFE OF MEANING

There's a wonderful book entitled *Man's Search for Meaning*, by Viktor Frankl. It describes a man who survived the brutal experiences of several concentration camps during World War ll. Despite the agony he endured, he survived because he wanted his life to have meaning. When your life has purpose and meaning, you find yourself with an inner energy that is unstoppable! If you don't know what your purpose is, then you're just wandering around being lost.

So, ask yourself, "Why am I really here?" And, "What would give my life meaning?"

> *"The more meaningful your life is, the happier and more excited about the future you will be."*

HOPE

You can't live without hope. It's what keeps us going. It makes us believe that anything is still possible. We are naturally attracted to positive, hopeful, and optimistic people because that's our nature.

These eight human needs are constantly working to fulfill themselves, and only when these are satisfied will you be able to focus all your energy and power to achieving your ideas, dreams, or goals.

SUCCESS IN SHOWBUSINESS IS NOT AN ACCIDENT

"A high-quality life starts with a high-quality you!"

To become successful in your acting career, I believe that you must also live as a successful person *in your own life*. I have learned that actors, performers, and business innovators who are successful in their own life always have the best chance to be successful in their careers. I've witnessed this happening repeatedly! This may surprise you, but it's true!

A successful person never complains about a lack of opportunities; they simply keep creating them. Some acting schools teach the idea that pursuing the acting profession will bring you a life of suffering, pain, and unhappiness. Who wants that? I consider that to be bad training. Actors who are taught how to act without being taught how to succeed in this business will surely fail. If you don't teach artists how to succeed, they won't.

Success also comes when you create a plan with deadlines and you actively meet them. Create a business model for yourself to remain accountable. Take the things you know you should do and make them happen. Next, sign up for reputable classes in acting, improv, dance, and singing. Prepare to film an incredible acting reel. And get great headshots with a top photographer. Depending on where you are in your career, these goals will continually change and evolve. Now, don't stress if it takes longer to achieve these goals than you anticipated—but an actor without a target will be unemployed. Remember, a dream without a plan is just a dream.

"Success is not an accident; it's a learned skill."

I chose to pursue the performing arts when I was in high school. I started my training in New York City, studying to become a professional performer. I have since become an actor, singer, dancer, screenwriter, producer, director, acting teacher, presenter, life coach, and business trainer. I have learned to become all these things because of my twenty-nine years of training with legendary teachers, mentors, and coaches, and because of the professional experiences I've had while touring in Broadway musicals, films, and TV shows. I have also coached executives and CEOs on how to become dynamic public speakers while giving keynote speeches at conferences. I have always had a tremendous appetite for learning; it feeds my soul! I continue to explore, research, and study daily.

These experiences have gone beyond my wildest expectations and have given me such a rich and purposeful life. I will be forever grateful for everyone that I have learned from and performed with. And a big thank-you to Eric Morris, whose work has always inspired me.

When I first started teaching, I read a quote from the legendary acting coach Uta Hagen. She said, "Acting is the worst-taught subject on the planet." I began to understand what she meant.

Actors who do not have a clear grasp of the craft or the business of showbusiness eventually will have their dreams turn into nightmares! Some are not even aware that their acting must continue to improve and develop because the audience constantly demands more from the actors.

Unfortunately, there are acting schools here and around the world that are not teaching the latest acting techniques and are therefore producing actors of the past. Sadly, they will not have a chance to be employed in this industry. Nobody wants to see people *act* anymore. The audience wants to see the actors *be* the part, not play the part. They want to see a vulnerable, emotional, truthful, and connected human being.

The right teacher will wake you up to your magnificent, creative, and powerful self! I know that fixing your underlying problems will give you the opportunity to discover what your career and life could really be like. Greatness is not something that only the lucky few are destined to achieve. Greatness is a choice that YOU have to make! It's something we are all capable of, but sadly, most don't do enough to go after it. I know that you have been put on this earth with limitless potential, and you could leave a big artistic mark on this world. Only when you realize your own self-worth will you achieve this. The techniques and methods in this book will provide you with a way to facilitate great performances. They might even help you one day win an Academy Award!

"You can have anything you want if you are willing to give up the belief that you can't have it." —Robert Anthony

CHAPTER 32

HOLLYWOOD—WHERE DREAMERS COME TO SUCCEED

"What got you here won't get you there."

Hollywood is the ultimate destination that filmmakers, actors, directors, and artists—from around the world—have been dreaming about for over a century. Every day, some of the best actors and artists come to Hollywood with the hope to succeed. If you want to work with the very best, Hollywood is the place to be.

Unfortunately, most people who come here don't succeed. Why is that? Well, there are two reasons. It's because they have never learned the "Rules of Hollywood" and never found a mentor who could show them what Hollywood expects from its actors and artists.

The rules below will make all the difference in succeeding in this industry.

RULE 1: "WHAT WILL I GIVE?" NOT "WHAT WILL I GET?"

Most people come to LA to get things. Hollywood will not respond to you unless you are ready to give something. The people in this industry can see this needy energy and sense of entitlement instantly. Trust me! The more you're willing to *share*, *offer*, and *present*, the more excited and interested people will be in you. Come with a giving mindset.

RULE 2: HOLLYWOOD RUNS ON ENERGY

If you don't have positive energy radiating out of your body, you will be unemployed because energy is Hollywood's currency. The successful artists I have met, for the most part, are very nice, professional, and have the energy I want to be around. Enthusiastic behavior will attract the right people into your career and life. George Clooney once said, "I wouldn't want to work with anyone who I couldn't have dinner with." You need to bring your best to everyone you encounter. Hollywood is like a dinner party. People don't want to spend four months on a set with someone who is unhappy, uninspired, or self-centered. That would be crazy! Artists who are thoughtful, kind, and keep improving themselves will attract more of the same. Enthusiastic behavior attracts the right people to your life and career.

RULE 3: YOU NEVER ATTRACT THE PERSON YOU WANT—YOU ATTRACT WHO YOU ARE

If you are a superficial person and you come to Hollywood, you're going to meet a lot of superficial people. In life, you always meet the kind of person you are. If you have negative friends then you had better look at yourself, because like attracts like. Positive people will meet other positive people. You must be the type of person you're looking for!

I am fully aware that there's a different side to Hollywood as well—a darker side. Now, if you keep encountering these kinds of people all the time, then you need to ask yourself, "Why am I meeting people like this? What changes do I need to make in myself to attract the people I want to work with?" We don't live in the world of our wishes. We live in a world we attract, create, build, and nurture.

"If you don't value yourself, you will always be attracted to people who don't value you either." —Sabrina Alexis

RULE 4: LIVE YOUR AUTHENTICITY

Be courageous enough to be your true self. This is not an easy thing to do, because many people tell you that who you are will never be good enough. Renowned artists share their authentic selves with the world. Know that your true self will keep progressing because you learn, grow, and expand.

"Be YOU—because everyone else is taken!"

RULE 5: BE PROACTIVE, NOT REACTIVE.

Hollywood admires people who don't sit around and complain or blame others. Hollywood likes artists who create their own opportunities and take their career and destiny into their own hands. It likes people who develop their own projects. The business has changed. It's now easier than ever to make your own projects using the latest technology. There are now film festivals screening iPhone movies. It is not enough to just be "an actor." You must be proactive; a true artist doesn't need to be told to create. To have more control over their career, some actors have also become directors, writers, and producers. So, get busy!

There are no other cities more open to foreign actors than Hollywood. Anyone from any country can get nominated for an Academy Award and win. Actors like Javier Bardem, Penélope Cruz, and Roberto Benigni have found success here. In 2020, the South Korean film *Parasite* won for Best Picture. That's outstanding! Hollywood recognizes greatness from everywhere!

RULE 6: BE GRATEFUL.

One of the things that Hollywood likes is gratitude. It embraces people who appreciate others for their effort and kindness. I have noticed that stars and other successful people in this industry are thankful to others for helping them. I find that most of the people at the top are caring individuals. They tell me that they feel fortunate to have a job and grateful to be in this business. Most realize that it's not just about being a *star*, but how they can help the world. I must say that I am very proud to come from an industry that makes such a difference by supporting charities, advocating for the environment, and highlighting social injustices.

RULE 7: CONNECT WITH YOUR HUMANITY.

You must be able to inspire others with your words, ideas, and humanity so that they will want to work with you. You have to learn how to build bridges with others. It's easy to build a wall, but it's difficult to build a bridge. Go to screenings, attend lectures, volunteer, get involved in meaningful causes. Just get out there! You never know who you are going to meet and what you can share with each other.

RULE 8: BECOME THE PERSON YOU HAVE NEVER BEEN.

You will have to give up your negative thinking, actions, and behaviors. Only when you become a greater version of yourself will your dreams be within your reach.

"If you want to achieve what you have never achieved, you have to become the person you have never been."

RULE 9: ASK FOR HELP.

You can't be successful alone. It's not possible. A baby is born asking for help, but they don't stop there. Successful people always ask for help;

average people don't. You must build a strong artistic community of friends, coaches, colleagues, and artists to help you. Everything that I have learned, I learned from someone willing to share their knowledge with me. I will be forever grateful, for I could not have succeeded without their help. To achieve anything extraordinary, you have to surround yourself with a lot of powerful collaborators. You can't make a great film alone. Be articulate and passionate about your vision. Everybody wants to be involved in a project that has meaning and purpose. Have a personality that people want to be around. Infect them with your energy, passion, humor, and love. This will make them want to get involved.

RULE 10: YOUR "WHY" HAS TO BE STRONGER THAN YOUR "FEARS." (*THE MOST IMPORTANT RULE*)

Successful artists make it because they have a *strong, meaningful,* and *emotional* WHY.

They are not doing this just for them, but for something bigger and more meaningful than themselves. Your "WHY" is also your mission statement. (Read more in chapter thirty-four: "Look Out, World!") Don't ever have a Plan B. When you only have a Plan A, you will have to succeed because you have no other option. Know that a lot of work, training, failing, and growing will need to happen to reach your visualized goals.

NOTE: Rules don't mean that you can't present your work and ideas in a totally different, original, and unpredictable way.

"I never dreamed about success. I worked for it." —*Estée Lauder*

"You cannot stop anyone with the right attitude, and you cannot help anyone with the wrong attitude."

CHAPTER 33

TRANSFORMATIONAL EXERCISES

Profound changes only come when you are pushed, encouraged, and have supportive guidance.

I have created exercises over the years that I use in my workshops, seminars, and Masterclasses. I am proud to say that they are now being taught by other acting coaches and trainers in other countries. I designed them to help actors, performers, and artists eliminate their blocks, doubts, and fears so they may discover their true, authentic selves. Afterward, my students and actors have increased their inner power and emotional connections and have experienced joyous freedom and the confidence to pursue the goals they have always dreamed of.

The exercises below could change your career if you let them!

MORNING MIRACLE EXERCISE

Each morning, stand in front of a mirror where you can see your body.

Look deeply into your eyes. Take your time, and take three deep breaths. Now, tense up your entire body. Bring every part of your body tightly together, and hold it for fifteen seconds—then relax it. Do this three times. You need to be truly relaxed for this exercise to work.

Now, look into the mirror and mentally send the person that you see a message, saying, "I want to connect with you more." Then slowly and quietly find it in your heart to say "I . . . love . . . you." Say it a few times. Sweetly and kindly. Now, start saying words to yourself that you've been *waiting to hear all your life*, gradually getting louder and louder and with more power.

Choose loving and supportive words, such as, "You are special, caring, kind, unique, beautiful, talented, extraordinary, brave, and destined for greatness," and so on. Do this for about eight minutes.

If you say it with emotional positive energy, it will affect you. Then, say all the things in your life that you are grateful for. Really think about it. The more you say, the better the outcome.

Then say all the things you are grateful for that *haven't* happened yet. For example, "Thank you for the incredible and exciting job that I'm going to start." And, "Thank you for all the opportunities and the miracles I will be experiencing." And, "I am so grateful for all the money that is coming my way." Or, "Thank you for that amazing romantic partner I'm going to meet." When you finish, take three deep breaths to feel energized and renewed.

Then, add five more minutes to the exercise, giving yourself a rousing pep talk, telling yourself with all your power, energy, and determination what an amazing day you are going to have and that you will triumph and overcome all barriers, problems, and obstacles.

Then say, with even more passion, "I'm so lucky to be me!" Commit to those words—over and over again—and say them loudly until you are convinced. "I'M SO LUCKY TO BE ME!" Only when you are convinced that you have the things you desire will you radiate the energy to attract them.

"I FEEL" EXERCISE

You can't just use a few keys on a piano to create a masterpiece; you need every key—the low notes and the high notes. Your emotions function in the exact same way. You must connect to them in order to be fully alive.

This exercise was designed to push you past your emotional limitations if you totally commit to it. Only when you can express all your emotions and feelings freely will you become a powerful and unstoppable actor or performer. So, I challenge you to do it full out. Be in a space where you can scream, and allow your emotions to get out of your body and be physically expressive.

Face a long mirror in a relaxed standing position but with full energy. Take slow, deep breaths. Start by disconnecting from your mind and connecting to your body and soul. Say quietly at first, "I . . . feel . . ." Keep repeating these two words until you express how you feel—not how you think. This is a stream of consciousness exercise, so keep talking. Most people have had their feelings trapped in their bodies for far too long. "I feel confused. I feel anxious. I feel lost. I feel happy. I feel stupid." Continue deepening this emotional connection and expressing your feelings for another eight minutes. Shock yourself by saying things that you have never said before. Don't explain WHY you feel this way; just express how you feel, and don't judge it. Then take a pause for a few minutes.

Then say, "I'm angry about . . ." and list all the things you are really angry about. Especially mention things that happened to you in your childhood. Do that for about eight minutes. Say it as *angrily* as possible, and scream from your innermost being, to free you from your pain and mental blocks!

Then say, "I'm sad about . . ." and mention all the things you are heartbroken about. Take a moment to connect with the sadness in your soul and your body *before you start.* Say everything and anything that comes to mind. Do that for eight minutes. Then breathe, and be silent for a few minutes.

Then say what you are planning to give to the world. "I'm going to give . . . my talent, my passion, my love, my energy, my heart, my creativity." Do that for eight minutes. Tell the world what they should be expecting from you. When you give something of value, you will get something of value. Afterward, jump up and down; feel excited and joyful about what you are going to give to the world.

Then, with tremendous power, pound on your chest, and, with your hand stretched out, say out loud: "My name is _____, and HERE I AM . . . AND THIS IS ME!!!" Say these words three times, and get bigger and louder every time you say them! Convince yourself that it's GREAT to be you! Then, jump up high three times and say, "HERE I AM . . . AND THIS IS *ALL* OF ME!"

NOTE: These exercises are more extensive and powerful in my classes.

Do these exercises three times a week, and you will noticeably see a new and improved you in the mirror.

RECONNECT TO YOUR HEART!

Good news! I found your soul mate. I'll bet you'll never guess who it is. It's YOU!

You are your soul mate! You will be with yourself more than any other partner in your life. Have the courage to start living in your heart, and your envisioned life can begin.

HEART MEDITATION EXERCISE

If you want to reconnect to your heart, sit silently in a quiet space, put your hand on your heart for five minutes, and listen to your breathing. Try to identify what your body is feeling right now. Where is the tension? Where is the pain? What is your body trying to tell you? Become a detective and discover your body's messages.

After that, tell your heart, "I need to connect to you." Ask, "What messages do you have for me?" Then, ask your heart four questions:

"What do you want me to know today?" Be still and listen for the answer . . .

"What's the most loving thing I should do for myself today?"

"What action step should I take next?" Listen to your instincts for the answers; they are speaking to you . . .

"Who do I need to contact that would help me?"

Every time you do this exercise, you could ask different questions.

Your heart and instincts are always speaking. If you have a turbulent mind, your inner voice is drowned out, and it becomes nothing more than a faint whisper. Sit in gratitude, and thank your heart and soul. Your heart has always been talking to you, but you haven't been listening. When you practice this, your inner voice will get louder! Your inner voice will put you on the right path.

EMOTIONAL BOOSTER EXERCISE

When you disconnect from your emotions, you become serious, boring, frozen, closed, and predictable. Emotional people have more fun! Joyous energy connects you to your emotions.

I want you to do something every day that brings you joy and fun. That's right; you need to have lots of fun! Go into nature; walk barefoot to ground yourself; watch a funny movie; eat pizza, ice cream, or chocolate cake! Anything that inspires you in a joyous way is what you must do.

Do things that bring you more laughter! Try something new and connect with people you love. Put on music and DANCE. Some people say, "Dance like no one's watching," but I like to say, "*Dance like EVERYONE'S watching!*"

Sadly, my students, clients, and artists are not having enough enjoyment! Living in your head makes you feel weak, insecure, and sad. When you are living in joy and gratitude, you are connected to the power of your heart. A contented heart attracts miracles and people that will inspire and help you along the way!

THREE PEOPLE EXERCISE

As I mentioned before, you learn most by doing. ACTION moves you forward. It is the key to life!

Start by calling three people and thank them for being in your life. Tell them how grateful you are to them for being there for you.

Then call three people who you've been having issues with and say, "I'm calling to see if we could possibly solve our problem." These are difficult calls to make, but this builds character, courage, and confidence. It confirms that you can accomplish difficult tasks when you have to.

Finally, call three people and ask them to be in your life. These important calls will move your life and career forward.

"Hard work beats talent—when talent doesn't work hard." —*Tom Notke*

My exercises are designed to help you reach new heights. They are empowering, creative, enriching, fun, and transformational. I would like to share them with you in my online or in my live Masterclasses.

Being guided and encouraged will push you further and deeper into accessing your talent. This will break through internal blocks to help you become the actor you must be to succeed. You will also discover new emotions, confidence, and power that you will be able to use in your work and life.

CHAPTER 34

LOOK OUT, WORLD!

*"Be a citizen of the planet and change the world
for the better." —Marlon Brando*

In my classes, I ask my students to tell me how the world would benefit from their success as an actor or artist. Truthfully, most people look a bit confused with the question. The general response is, "Well, I just want to work. That's all." But I always remind them that to be successful in showbusiness, or any business, the audience or public must benefit from what they are offering. Every product becomes successful when others recognize the high value that you add to their endeavor or life.

How does your talent or skill benefit others?

What value are you bringing to the world with your abilities, ideas, or experiences? Are you here to give inspiration, knowledge, guidance, love, hope, or joy to others? Maybe it's to show people like you, who were also told that they could never achieve anything special, that they can, by seeing *your* success.

Are you willing to share your personal life stories, allowing others to feel less embarrassed or ashamed about their own?

Do you want to create a film, documentary, or a play that brings focus to an injustice and gives it much-needed attention?

"I believe that artists can change the world with their art, talent, and voice. For me, they are the gladiators of life. Artists have always made a big difference in this world."

So, I ask you this important question: "Why does the world need YOU to become an artist? What are you going to bring?" There's a desperate need in all human beings to ease the loneliness of existence by creating a bond with other people through shared experiences, thoughts, and feelings. Thereby, we experience a deeper level of connection, ending isolation and gaining the opportunity to share our authentic selves with everyone in the world.

We have to realize that, despite physical appearances, we are all fundamentally the same in our desires. Art transcends all races, gender, language, religion, politics, and cultures. Through art, we share our pain, fears, dreams, hopes, loves, joys, greed, fantasies, and triumphs. When we watch a play, see a film, or listen to a song that resonates with our soul, we feel as though someone understands us.

> ## *"Compassion, empathy, and a deeper understanding of others will heal our world."*

In my opinion, this is the most compelling gift that we can give to each other. Holding back your gifts or talent is a tragedy. Acting is part of a living tradition, a legacy that must be guarded and maintained with absolute ferocity. I am so grateful that I've been given the gift to be a performer, artist, and teacher.

If you've been given the gift to be an actor or performer, consider yourself lucky! Sometimes people will tell you that being an actor or performer is not a "real" job. You know what? They're right! It's not a real job. *It's the greatest job!* I feel that we are "*the doctors for the soul.*" Actors share their heart, their life, and their humanity—which is brave. It's time to let your skills and brilliance shine brighter than ever before!

> *"If you live a great life, when you look back, you'll be able to enjoy it a second time."* —Dalai Lama

CHAPTER 35

NO TIME TO WASTE, PROCRASTINATE, OR DELAY

When you realize that you have a limited amount of time, you will appreciate your family, friends, dreams, and your life a lot more.

Too many of us think that we have plenty of time, and this is the biggest mistake you can make in life. We say, "One day I'll . . ." There is no *one day*. There is only **NOW**.

Many people make excuses, such as, "It's not the right moment," or "I'm not ready." The time you're killing is just killing you. You are waiting for life to take the first step, but only when you have the courage to act will life *react* and provide you with the necessary tools, lessons, and opportunities you will need to fulfill your goals.

"You can't have a better tomorrow if you are still stuck on yesterday."

Time has no remorse. It doesn't care if you're young, old, or if you've lived a full and happy life or hardly lived at all. It will cut you short whenever it pleases, and it has no shame in not giving you a warning when it's about to end. It doesn't matter how rich you are or how much money you make. You can always make more money, but you can never make more time.

"Time is the most valuable thing in the universe."

Time is more valuable than diamonds. Only when you realize how priceless it really is will you abandon your blocks, fears, sadness, and regrets, and go after the life you truly desire!

> *"The bad news is time flies. The good news is you're the pilot."* —Michael Altshuler

Here are some important suggestions in using the time you have left to achieve your goals and dreams.

ACCEPT LOVE

Don't deny love when it finds you; be open to grasp it fully, and let it in.

"Life is too short to be at war with yourself!"

INCREASE YOUR SELF-WORTH

You must get into a state of high self-worth. This will force you to act and believe in your specialness, which allows you to start pursuing extraordinary things.

> *"Know that developing your talent and not increasing self-love is a waste."*

You have been put on this earth to achieve greatness—if you choose it.

START WRITING

Write down the things that you're passionate about. Don't just think about it, write them down. Then you'll know what's truly important and you'll focus your energy there. When you write things down *with target dates*, you can manifest your ideas and goals into the physical world.

> *"You must use your time creatively . . . to do great things."* —*Martin Luther King Jr.*

LISTEN TO YOUR DISCERNING HEART

Stop wasting time overanalyzing the situation, and act on what your heart or instinct is telling you to do next. Heart messages come from a higher power. Trust, and go for it!

TIME IS A GIFT CALLED "PRESENT"!

Reach out to those you love today, and tell them how much they mean to you. Do the things today that you have been avoiding. Share your gifts and talents, contact someone to coach or help you, or create a project with them. The outcome will surprise you.

> *"What you are going to do next is the most important moment in your life."*

Capture all of life's important, special moments as if you are the camera. Don't take "pictures" of things that are not important. Don't just exist in this world, but fully LIVE IN IT. Time stops for no one.

> *"You don't have to stay up all night to succeed. You just have to be fully awake during the day!"*

CHAPTER 36

YOU'VE GOT A PARACHUTE

When artists or actors embark on actualizing their life goals or dreams, it seems daunting, unrealistic, impossible, and, of course, unattainable. That's a logical belief, but to pursue your dreams is to fully comprehend that all dreams will bring you to the cliff's edge. You will have to be ready to jump off!

I understand that you may be afraid because you feel that if you do jump you could certainly fall to your death. However, what you don't know is that we were all born with an invisible parachute on our backs. Yep, that's right! Which will only open once you find the courage to jump. Be aware that the parachute does not open immediately. So, don't panic, and have faith that it will open!

"Faith activates miracles—and fear activates your negativity!"

If your current circumstances and negative thinking paralyze you while you are on top of your cliff, then you must be courageous and take this leap of faith right now. Know that nothing great or exceptional will ever happen until you take that risk. I promise you—you will gain 200 percent more out of life by taking that leap rather than standing on the cliff's edge waiting, overthinking, and letting those opportunities pass you by. It takes courage to believe that you will survive your jump, but you will. This is the only way anyone has ever discovered what their future has in store for them or what their life could be.

Embracing uncertainty requires faith in the unknown and, more importantly, faith in YOU. This can seem scary, but the real torment is letting your fears and doubts stop you from fulfilling your potential and deepest desires. It also keeps you from experiencing the incredible life that was meant for you. The thought of you never living your true life is heartbreaking to me.

"F.A.I.T.H. Stands for Finding Answers in the Heart!"

Let your dreams carry you into uncharted territory to help you build a more glorious life for yourself. This is the moment to take the chance of a lifetime and believe in your goals and your instincts. Love yourself enough to know that your parachute will open. Low self-worth and the lack of self-love are devastating problems facing the world.

This book is designed to give you the tools, methods, and transformational techniques to achieve what is perceived as impossible. Success only comes to those who are courageous enough to take the LEAP!

These situations may put you into a crisis, but remember, you're in a crisis so that you can become the hero of your own life!

This is your moment to become the HERO! The Chinese word for *crisis* has two characters, which signify danger and opportunity: 危機.

This is your opportunity to become the actor, performer, or creative artist you've always dreamt you could be.

> *"The reason we exist is to make a difference in this world."*

CHAPTER 37

READY TO START LIVING YOUR DREAM?

"A dream is like being pregnant. How well you take care of your baby's needs will determine the success of your dream."

Know that your dreams are not supposed to be an escape from everyday reality. Dreams were given to you so you could fulfill your destiny. It was a gift from the creator, and this is the reason you are here on earth!

My mentor Wayne Dyer taught me, "Start before you're ready, and never let money stop you."

If you want to become the actor or performer you have always dreamt of—START NOW!

If you are serious about becoming a great actor, you should visit Los Angeles at least once to experience the energy of this wonderful city. The elites and those who want to work with the top professionals come here to study, grow, and create. Hollywood is the Olympics for acting, or as I like to say, "It's the Olympics for the Olympics!" Hollywood is full of pressure and excitement, but real artists love pressure. They want to become *elite* actors. THE BEST IN THE WORLD!

If you want to be one of the greatest actors, then there is a lot of work that needs to be done, but I know you can achieve anything if you have the right mindset, passion, and acting techniques. Success comes from allowing yourself to be: Open | Emotional | Vulnerable | Determined.

PROTECT YOUR DREAM—IT IS WHAT YOU WERE BORN TO DO!

It is important that you have a great mentor that you can fully resonate with because you will need someone to help you figure out what's going wrong and what's going right. It is not possible to do this by yourself. You will need an expert to take you to the highest level.

> *"A dream you dream alone is only a dream. A dream you dream together is reality." —John Lennon*

Remember, dreams or goals without deadlines are just wishes.

TURN YOUR DREAMS INTO REALITY

You must have an effective plan for how you will create your long-lasting acting career. Benjamin Franklin once said, "If you fail to plan, you plan to fail." Eventually, you will need private sessions with a mentor you trust, who can help you create the plan that's just right for you. The road to success is different for everyone. So, there is not just one given plan to follow. You will have to create one. Reading this book will not only benefit your career and life, but encourage you to change the world in some profound and lasting way.

> *"Don't give up on your dreams, or your dreams*
> *will give up on you." —John Wooden*

Know that if you take the lessons from this book to heart and put them into action, it will bring you to the success that you have always wanted. You are now equipped with tactics, strategies, techniques, stories, and methods that my actors and artists have used and continue to succeed with. It's time for you to become the star in your own career and life!

> **"The greatest training in the world**
> **will only work—if you use it."**

Some people do the same thing in exactly the same way forever. This leads to an extremely dull, boring, and painful life. Adventure, fun, and excitement emanate from change. If you reject change, incredible experiences and life-changing opportunities will pass you by. Change is happening to you every day; it's unavoidable. It's something you will need to work on for the rest of your life.

You must also find fellow travelers who are passionate supporters along the way.

Only through change will you become the artist and human being you need to be to succeed. There is no other way!

> **"Only by changing your life will you
> know how powerful you can be."**

Know that the future will be better than the past and that vulnerability is the most important ingredient for your life and career.

Mother Teresa said, "I am a pencil in the hand of God." You also have the power to write a new and exciting chapter for yourself full of passion, love, purpose, and success. May this moment be the beginning of a brilliant new day in your miraculous life.

A FINAL STORY ABOUT YOU!

As a tiny child, you wore a small coat, and as you grew up, your parents had to buy you a bigger coat because you were getting bigger. A snake does the same thing with its own skin: it must shed its original skin to grow. If you are feeling unhappy, unsatisfied, or uncomfortable, it's because you are still wearing that tiny coat that doesn't fit you anymore.

You've grown emotionally and spiritually. So, it's time to throw that restrictive coat away and try on something new that fits perfectly! The most generous thing a person can ever do is to share their gifts, talents, humor, love, hope, joy, and their humanity with the world.

"You can't be serious about acting or your dream if you don't do something major for your career every day!"

A PERSONAL MESSAGE

There will be times when people will give you a negative assessment of your chances of succeeding with your goals and dreams. You have to remember that they are projecting onto you how they would feel about trying to reach that goal or dream themselves, because no one knows what *you* are capable of. They are just talking about what *they* would be able to accomplish. Don't let their negative projection affect your positive outcome.

One of the sheer joys that I have in my life is seeing my actors, singers, performers, and clients use what I've taught them to propel themselves to the top of their profession. As you continue moving forward, pursuing your goals, remember that you are standing on the shoulders of giants. They are your ancestors and the people who came before you—the ones who are no longer with us. Take a moment and reflect on everything they have sacrificed so that you may pursue your dreams. They're all rooting for you!

If you allow them to inspire you, they will guide you because they know something you may have forgotten—YOU are the "chosen one."

Regardless of who you are or where you're from, your dreams are possible. I feel it's your responsibility to give your unique greatness to the world.

"When you betray yourself, you are no different from the people who hurt you."

I'd like to share a very powerful story with you that I will never forget.

The great Indian activist Mahatma Gandhi had just spoken in a small village about freedom from British rule. He was leaving to go back to the train when a newspaper reporter asked him a question: "What message do you have for my people?" He paused for a moment and said, "My life is my message." What a powerful statement! Gandhi was a man who made it his life's mission to live a courageous and authentic life.

"If the way you live your life is YOUR message, what are you telling the world?"

I'm always thinking about my relatives and friends who are no longer here, as they inspire me to keep going. I have strived to live my life as artistically and authentically as possible. I am so grateful that the performing arts exist, and it's given me the most enriching, adventurous, interesting, and fulfilling life. I feel blessed.

Whatever you do right now—that's your message to the world.

"Your life is a work of art, and how you live, speak, and act is the artistic legacy you leave behind."

WISHING YOU A SUCCESSFUL AND INCREDIBLE JOURNEY!

I look forward to meeting you.

With never-ending love and encouragement,

Bernard Hiller

David Oyelowo, *Selma*, shares his wisdom and artistry with the LA International Masterclass.

Photo: Jordan Engle

ACKNOWLEDGMENTS

This book is dedicated to all the people who make a difference in the world. I am so thankful to all the wonderful people, some of whom I may never know—the ones who care, give, help, love, share their talent, speak up against injustice, and show up in times of need, even for people they don't know. Kindness and empathy toward others have always inspired me.

"How wonderful it is that nobody needs to wait a single moment before starting to improve the world." —Anne Frank

I especially want to thank my wonderful, loving, and supportive parents, Dewoire and Yossel Hiller, who taught me to bring love to others and to make the world a better place. They were Holocaust survivors who endured tremendous suffering, while losing most of the members of their families. Throughout it all, they gave me all the encouragement that I could ever have wished for. The confidence that they instilled in me made me feel like I could accomplish anything, and they helped me make my dreams and goals possible.

A special thank-you to my talented children, Dora and David, who made me become a better person and father. They bring me love and laughter whenever we are together. I also want to thank the mother of my children, Winnie, for encouraging me to first begin teaching, and especially my niece Rachel, who helped me write my first book. I'm so appreciative of my brother, Jaime, and my extended family in New York. To my beautiful, extraordinary, and inspiring sister, Golda, my heartfelt gratitude for your wisdom and for standing by me and cheering me on. Your presence in my life means so much to me. I love you all!

I'm also grateful to Sean Patrick for his support. To the extraordinary Terry Samaras, a life coach and business trainer, and Sarah Ross, an executive coach and my concept editor, both of whom have helped me shape the book that I have always wanted to write.

A massive thank-you to my editors and dear friends: Dustin Kerls, Adrian Gaeta, and Sandra De Sousa. It has been an honor having you on this journey with me. Your knowledge as actors, writers, and coaches has been invaluable in bringing this book to life. I could not have done this without all of you!

OUR TEAM

There's a question that people always wonder about: "What's more important, the journey or the destination?" And the answer is, "It's the COMPANY you're with."

I want to give special thanks to my amazing team, who create our incredible classes, Masterclasses, workshops, and seminars around the world. They are talented, devoted, and passionate organizers, assistants, and coaches. To all of you that I work with, I feel very lucky to know you, and I learn every time I'm with you.

A heartfelt thanks to all our videographers, especially Adrian Grand. You can see their extraordinary work on our website.

I am forever grateful to Antonio Cantos, Sonia Dorado, Jenna Manning, Dan Hubbard, Farid Madour, Giulio Benvenuti, Laura Ruocco, Marco Iannone, Paolo Chiesa, Julia Bähre, Nicky Gerzabek, Peter Windhofer, Nicoleta Ciobanu, Nikolaus Schmid, Vanessa Rancourt, Maimouna Coulibaly, Palmer Davis, Anna Sergushkina, Jesus Schettino, Peter Augustin, Connor Shelefontiuk, Aki Avni, Jackie Lewis, April Webster, Dustin Kerls, Adrian Gaeta, and Sandra De Sousa. You have been instrumental in creating our transformational events. Thank you for all your energy, hard work, love, and advice.

I also would like to thank my instincts; I could not be here without you.

This is the end of the beginning . . .

ABOUT THE AUTHOR

BERNARD HILLER—CEO & ARTISTIC DIRECTOR

Bernard (Bernardo) Hiller was born in Buenos Aires, Argentina, lived in Germany, and then moved to New York City. After attending the High School of Performing Arts and the Alvin Ailey Dance Studio, he became a professional actor, singer, and dancer, performing in Broadway musicals that toured the US and opera houses across Europe.

Bernard has been a transformational leader in the field of artistic performance, dynamic communication, and success strategies for the past twenty-eight years. He has coached actors and artists such as Jeff Goldblum, Cameron Diaz, Lionel Richie, LL Cool J, Lindsay Lohan, Jamie Dornan, Vanessa Hudgens, Michael Bolton, A. R. Rahman, Nadja Swarovski, Emilio Rivera, Emma Roberts, Jennifer Garner, Billy Crystal, Chace Crawford, and many more. Bernard also teaches his acting methods to Opera singers in Venice, Los Angeles, New York, Florence, and London. He has been a jury member at several film festivals around the world and has written major motion picture screenplays. He is a producer on several films and TV projects.

Bernard also coaches Fortune 500 CEOs and executives to accelerate their success. He will be writing his next book using his unique methods and techniques for business leaders.

Technology has made Bernard even more accessible through his online training. He trains actors in LA and around the world, including Rick Cosnett (from Australia) in *The Vampire Diaries*, Fernando Cayo (from Spain) in *La Casa de Papel—Money Heist*, Ehan Bhat (from India) in *99 Songs*, Roxane Duran (from France) in *Marie Antoinette*, and Shira Haas (from Israel) in *Unorthodox* and *Shtisel*. Russian-born actor Costa Ronin came to Bernard's classes to learn his dynamic techniques. Since then, Costa has starred in *The Americans* and *Homeland*. We are proud of all our artists that continue to use their talents and gifts in film, TV, and theatre.

Bernard also wishes to thank Samuel L. Jackson, Leonardo DiCaprio, Kenny Ortega, Deepak Chopra, and motivational trainer Les Brown for their gracious support of his work.

Bernard Hiller Acting & Success Studio

Los Angeles – London – Rome – Madrid

bernardhiller.com

ALSO BY BERNARD HILLER

Stop Acting, Start Living

CONTACT INFORMATION

Thank you for taking the time to read this book. To find out more about our methods, techniques, classes, and Masterclasses, please visit our website: www.bernardhiller.com.

Sign up to our newsletter for unique insight, information, and knowledge on how to create your success in this industry.

The newsletter is being read in over one hundred countries.

Please share your success stories with us:

- Instagram – bernard.hiller
- Facebook – Bernard Hiller Acting & Success Studio
- Contact: bernard@bernardhiller.com
- Private One-on-One Sessions & On-Set Coaching
- Business Training, Life Coaching & Dynamic Speaking Skills

Let Bernard speak and inspire your team at your next event!